"THAT'S WHAT SHE SAID!"

A GUIDE TO USING "THE OFFICE" TO DEMONSTRATE MANAGEMENT PARABLES, ORGANIZATIONAL BEHAVIOR AND HUMAN RESOURCE MANAGEMENT TOPICS IN THE MANAGEMENT CLASSROOM

BY

ROBERT G. DELCAMPO, PH.D., KRISTIE M. BOUDWIN and SHERRI L. HINES

The following is not a novelization or an actual script but a dry transcript of the aired episode that includes accurate word-to-word dialogues, settings descriptions, action scenes and/or camera movements where necessary. "THE OFFICE" and other related entities are owned, (TM) and © by REVEILLE PRODUCTIONS and NBC UNIVERSAL TELEVISION. This work is published without their permission, approval, authorization or endorsement. Any reproduction, duplication, distribution or display of this material in any form or by any means is expressly prohibited. It is absolutely forbidden to use for commercial gain. This work is intended for entertainment and educational purposes only. No infringement intended.

© Copyright 2007, Robert G. DelCampo, Ph.D., Kristie M. Boudwin and Sherri L. Hines

All Rights Reserved.

No part of this book may be reproduced, stored in a retrieval system, or transmitted by any means, electronic, mechanical, photocopying, recording, or otherwise, without written permission from the author.

ISBN: 978-1-4303-0844-7

Table of Contents

Table of Contents iii
Introduction v
What is "The Office?" 1
Cast of Characters 5
How-to-Use this Book 11
Episode-by-Episode Guide 13
    SEASON 1 15
        Episode 1 – Pilot 16
        Episode 2 – Diversity Day 20
        Episode 3 – Health Care 24
        Episode 4 – The Alliance 28
        Episode 5 – Basketball 31
        Episode 6 – Hot Girl 34
    SEASON 2 39
        Episode 2–1 The Dundies 40
        Episode 2–2 Sexual Harassment 44
        Episode 2–3 Office Olympics 48
        Episode 2–4 The Fire 52
        Episode 2–5 Halloween 56
        Episode 2–6 The Fight 60
        Episode 2–7 The Client 64
        Episode 2–8 Performance Review 68
        Episode 2–9 Email Surveillance 72
        Episode 2–10 Christmas Party 76
        Episode 2–11 Booze Cruise 80
        Episode 2–12 The Injury 84
        Episode 2–13 The Secret 88
        Episode 2–14 The Carpet 93
        Episode 2–15 Boys and Girls 97
        Episode 2–16 Valentine's Day 101
        Episode 2–17 Dwight's Speech 105
        Episode 2–18 Take Your Daughter To Work Day 109
        Episode 2–19 Michael's Birthday 113

  Episode 2–20 Drug Testing 117
  Episode 2–21 Conflict Resolution 121
  Episode 2–22 Casino Night 125
Bibliography 129
Index 131

Introduction

Increasingly, business educators use Hollywood films or television shows to concretize Organizational Behavior and Human Resource theories or principles (Champoux, 2001; Corner, 2001; Hunt, 2001). For example, Huczynski (1994) recommends the Magnificent Seven movie to illustrate how various needs in Maslow's need hierarchy motivate different characters. As competition for the attention of business school students becomes more and more competitive with the rise of cell phone usage, text messaging, iPods and the like; instructors must respond to student needs by making information as accessible and entertaining as possible. Educational psychology literature notes that creating an entertaining or interesting "cue" that is associated with a particular topic can improve student retention of subject matter. Herein lies the purpose of our text, to provide an entertaining AND educational exposition of difficult to grasp OB/HR topics. This demonstration not only makes the subject matter more accessible for students, it also creates the mental "cue" we discuss for improved recall and retention of these topics.

In watching NBC's "The Office," one can reflect on the common office-place interplay and recall their own, similar situations in their own work environments. How many times has a worker "goofed off" when the boss is out of the office, or played a potentially damaging "prank" on a co-worker? Herein lies the inspiration for this book. "The Office: An American Workplace" (as the pilot episode was originally titled) is a humorous and sometimes entirely too accurate portrayal of the American Workplace, and therein an ideal demonstration of many topics that are taught in today's business schools. Most obviously, topics of Organizational Behavior and Human Resource Management are demonstrated, but the list does not end there. The pedagogical use of "The Office" is not limited to the examples in this text but only by one's imagination.

This incorporation of contemporary media into the classroom can effectively contribute to management lessons (Champoux, 2001; Corner, 2001; Hunt, 2001). Seeing portrayals of corporate settings may be particularly helpful to students. "The Office" is a unique sitcom that presents a dysfunctional corporate setting in a comedic fashion. The presentation of a mock-corporate experience illustrates the violations of norms commonly taken for granted in a work setting. The show debuted on NBC in March of 2005 and is currently in its fourth season. "The Office" that is seen on NBC is an adaptation of the BBC version of the show, adjusted for the U.S. audience.

NBC's "The Office" is unique in that it portrays everyday office behavior as filmed through a "mockumentary" lens. The thrust of the series is around the exploits, managerial prowess (or lack thereof) and office relationships created by Dunder Mifflin Scranton Regional Manager Michael Scott (Steve Carrell). Dunder Mifflin is a regional paper supplier with limited resources trying to compete with national-level discount suppliers such as Staples, OfficeMax and the like. Michael's sales crew, accounting department and oft-dismissed HR representative (Toby) comprise the bulk of the case of "The Office".

Basic norms of the American work environment are tested in each episode. The Emmy Award winning sitcom develops unique characterizations through individual's actions in their work environment. The variety of characters offers viewers various perspectives on the work setting, where problems are prevalent and productivity is scarce.

Management textbooks offer explanations of topics and ideal work setting scenarios. This television show offers a learning experience from a different approach, clearly portraying what does not work to create a healthy and productive work environment. The violation of norms can be particularly helpful for teaching organizational behavior, as corporate culture and interpersonal relationships are central to understanding a work environment. This program can serve as a valuable tool to teach management topics that are difficult for students to grasp. Used properly, the sitcom can supplement more traditional instructional tools and enhance the learning experience.

What is "The Office?"

"The Office"—UK Version

Having premiered in 2000 to much critical acclaim (and winning an Emmy for Outstanding Comedy Program), the Slough branch of a paper company, Wernham Hogg, is the subject of an ongoing TV mockumentary (documentary style with sarcastic overtone). Cameras track the every move and offer one-on-one interviews of branch manager David Brent and his team as they go about their business (BBC, 2007).

"The Office"—US Version

Premiering in 2005, the US version of "The Office", just like the original, features a mock-u-doc-u-reality style of presentation. Instead of Wernham Hogg, the paper supply company is Dunder Mifflin Inc. of Scranton, Pennsylvania. Regional manager Michael Scott is the foil to David Brent, a middle-aged and a rather self-confident tour guide. Just like Brent, he is the office 'funnyman' and a fountain of "business wisdom" to his employees (BBC, 2007)

Cast of Characters

For the purpose of these teaching experiences, it is helpful to be familiar with the following main characters (while there are other ancillary characters, the bulk of the story lines surround the following):

Dwight Schrute: Dwight's title is "assistant to the regional manager." He is power hungry and jumps on any opportunity to take on more responsibility. Dwight seems to think he is superior to his coworkers; therefore he welcomes the idea of downsizing. Dwight often buys into Michael's "plans" and uses any power he achieves to torture co-workers, especially Jim. His overbearing tendencies and obsession with rules make his character particularly easy to antagonize for co-workers.

Jim Halpert: Jim is the underachieving sales representative whose lack of motivation seems to keep him with the company. Jim's intelligence and wit are revealed in his intimate friendship with receptionist Pam. Jim spends much of his time executing office pranks, particularly targeting Dwight.

Pam Beesly: Pam is the bashful receptionist whose is commonly frustrated with Michael's jokes and disregard for anything business related. When the show begins, Pam has been engaged to an employee in the warehouse for three years, but has a unique fondness for Jim.

Ryan Howard: Ryan is brought into the office as a temporary employee and sometimes referred to as "temp" by others in the office. He is usually sarcastic when interacting with employees and is very unenthusiastic about working at Dunder Mifflin. Ryan says he hopes to one day own his own business and tries to engage in the workplace as little as possible.

Jan Levinson-Gould: Jan is the supervisor that Michael reports to at the corporate office. Jan is very disapproving of Michael's jokes and management style, and spends much of their conversations scolding him for being inappropriate and ineffective.

Toby: Toby is the corporate appointed Human Resources representative for Dunder Mifflin in the Scranton branch. Michael commonly refers to Toby as "not part of their family" since he reports to the corporate office.

Oscar: Oscar works for Angela in the Accounting Department of the Scranton office. Oscar and Kevin commonly engage in inane and juvenile games to the chagrin on Angela. Oscar's sexuality and ethnic origin are commonly mocked by Michael.

Angela: Angela manages the Accounting Department in the Scranton branch and has a "secret" romantic relationship with Dwight. Angela is commonly referred to as "tight ass" and rarely expresses joy. She also regularly criticizes the shoddy work of Oscar and Kevin.

Kevin: Kevin is the third employee of the Accounting Department in the Scranton branch. Continually "trying" to be "cool," he makes many comments about the attractiveness of the female employees in the office. Kevin is also in a "Police" cover band.

Kelly: Kelly serves in a customer relations/customer service capacity in Scranton. She constantly talks and is

	despised by many for her logorrhea. Kelly is infatuated with Ryan "The Temp" and commonly discusses her desire to marry him and have children.
Todd Packer:	Todd is Michael's old sales buddy who commonly engages in inappropriate office talk and pranks. Todd commonly degrades and harasses the women in the office during his rare visits and is despised by many.
Meredith:	Meredith has a severe drinking problem and can commonly be seen having alcoholic beverages during work hours. While her exact role in Scranton is nebulous, it is commonly mentioned that she has many children and is divorced.
Creed:	Creed is from locations unknown. A member of the sales team, he has a distinctly odd take on life and is all consumed with furthering his own personal agenda no matter who gets in the way. Creed commonly shifts the blame for his many shortcomings to other Dunder Mifflin employees.
Devon:	Devon is most well-known for being "the person Michael fires". As a member of the sales team Devon is well liked but easy to fire as Michael believes he will not question his decision.
Stanley:	Stanley is an outstanding performer on the sales team. While never too motivated to take on any extra-role behaviors, he appears to be quite effective in selling to his niche of clients. Stanley is commonly ostracized by Michael through jokes about his racioethnic background.
Daryl:	Daryl runs the warehouse portion of the Dunder Mifflin Scranton Branch. While Michael believes

that he runs that portion of the business as well, he routinely folds under pressure from Daryl and his staff.

Roy: Roy is Pam's fiancée and an employee in the warehouse. Roy attempts to balance the needs of his fiancée and the need to participate in the misogynistic behaviors of the warehouse crew. His character develops as the series continues.

How-to-Use this Book

As you will see this text is organized into an episode-by-episode guide to the US version of NBC's "The Office". Each 22-minute (with the exception of some longer "special" episodes) episode description has:

Summary
    a summary of the plot points

Topics
    relevant OB/HR topics covered in the episode

Clip Description-Start/Stop
    detailed information about particularly poignant scenes with DVD time codes (to aid in use in the classroom)

Questions for Discussion
    (to start discussion about either specific portions of the episode or the episode as a whole)

"Answers to Look For" (italicized portion of discussion questions)
    in order to help the instructor either "pull out" move information from their students or to evaluate the quality of their responses. While these suggested responses hit on many OB/HR theories, they are not intended to be exhaustive of all of the possible quality responses from students.

Episode-by-Episode Guide

SEASON 1

ROBERT G. DELCAMPO, PH.D., KRISTIE M. BOUDWIN and SHERRI L. HINES

THE OFFICE
SEASON ONE

Episode 1 – Pilot

Summary: The head office of Dunder Mifflin advises Regional Manager Michael Scott that there will be downsizing in the near future. He promises his staff that there will be no firings. Ryan, the new temp, arrives at the office just in time to join in harassing Dwight and witnesses Michael's attempt to be funny and fire Pam for Post-It note theft.

Topics: Organizational Culture, Sexual Harassment, Co-Worker Harassment, Downsizing, Job Security

"THAT'S WHAT SHE SAID!"

Clip Description	**Start/Stop**
Michael makes an inappropriate sexual comment to Pam in front of the documentary crew while making introductions.	1:53 – 3:04
Co-worker harassment between Dwight and Jim.	8:52 – 9:49
Office meeting regarding potential downsizing. Michael promises that there will be no downsizing yet and is corrected by Pam. He makes an inappropriate comment to Stanley.	11:44 – 13:43
Jim has encased Dwight's stapler in jello. Michael and Ryan join Jim in making comments and harassing Dwight.	14:10 – 16:22
Michael "punks" Pam by telling her that she is being let go for Post-It note theft.	18:00 – 20:52

NOTES:

ROBERT G. DELCAMPO, PH.D., KRISTIE M. BOUDWIN and SHERRI L. HINES

Questions for Discussion:

1. Michael's tour at the beginning of the pilot serves as an introduction to the "Dunder Mifflin Stanton Branch." What observations can you make about the culture of the organization based on Michael's interaction with his employees?

    Responses from students will likely point out Michael's misguidance to Jim in the beginning of the episode and his inappropriate comment about Pam's appearance. These situations reveal components of the organizational culture, showing that Michael's skill set is not adequate for mentoring or managing his employees and also displays that various types of harassment are accepted in the work environment. When analyzing these situations, it may be helpful to ask students if these observations of the culture came from physical artifacts, explicitly stated values, or underlying assumptions.

2. Office humor becomes a part of many organizational cultures. In this episode, Jim and Dwight intentionally upset one another repeatedly. As a manager, where do you draw the line between office jokes and harassment? What is appropriate to joke about and what topics are off limits?

    Student responses will vary on this topic, as many students will see the jokes as funny while others may identify the behavior as inappropriate or counterproductive. It is important to point out that Michael joins in on the Jello prank played on Dwight. Later in the episode, Michael plays a joke of his own on Pam, telling her she is fired. As a manager, it is his responsibility to maintain a productive work environment where employees feel safe, but instead he is condoning behaviors associated with harassment.

3. After Michael's meeting with Jan reveals the possibility of downsizing, he assures his employees that they have nothing to worry about. Pam, who was also in the meeting, reveals that Michael does not have the authority to offer this reassurance. How does the work environment change after the downsizing possibility is revealed?

Responses will probably identify that employees are threatened by the job insecurity and realize they cannot trust their manager regarding the topic. Common behaviors associated with job insecurity are decreased commitment to the organization, decreased job satisfaction, heightened stress and lower levels of job involvement. It is important to identify the different employees' reactions to the downsizing rumors. Jan reveals her dislike for her current position and says it would not be the worst thing if this job no longer existed for her. Dwight is sure that he will not be let go and welcomes the competition.

ROBERT G. DELCAMPO, PH.D., KRISTIE M. BOUDWIN and SHERRI L. HINES

THE OFFICE
SEASON ONE

Episode 2 – Diversity Day

Summary: The "Racial Tolerance and Diversity in the Workplace" seminar is scheduled for the morning at Dunder Mifflin. The seminar was scheduled because of Michael's insensitivity and inappropriate behavior. Michael personally conducts a second seminar in the afternoon featuring racial charades involving the use of stereotypes to act out various ethnicities.

Topics: Diversity, Cultural Sensitivity, Stereotypes, Work Environment

Clip Description	Start/Stop
The morning session begins with Michael timing the exit of his office to coincide with Jim, the consultant. Michael undermines with interruptions and inappropriate comments. Michael suggests that "everybody say a race that you are attracted to sexually." The "Chris Rock routine" was the issue that bothered the employees and is reenacted.	3:27 – 7:56
The session resumes and all employees are requested to sign forms with Michael resisting. He finally signs with the name "Daffy Duck" and tears up the form in front of his staff. He informs the staff that there will be a second diversity training	7:57 – 12:04
Michael's diversity session begins. It includes racial charades using stereotypes to act out ethnicities and Michael making comments about the "negative connotations" of the term Mexican as well as comments about Arabs.	12:05 – 17:56
The session continues with Michael offending Kelly's Indian heritage by imitating an Indian convenience store owner.	18:17 – 19:23
The debriefing session is conducted by Michael who is still clueless and making offensive comments.	19:54 – 21:27

NOTES:
Both training sessions should be seen in their entirety.

Questions for Discussion:

1. Why wasn't the diversity training required by the corporate office a beneficial experience? Why is diversity a difficult topic for training?

> Students may suggest a variety of reasons that the training was not successful. Lack of cooperation and support from the manager sends the message to the employees that the issue is not important. Other students may suggest that the first training did not address the right issues or did not address them correctly. The person that was brought in to lead the diversity training did not seem to know his audience well, which would have helped him in selecting beneficial activities. Diversity is a difficult topic to confront because of the sensitivity surrounding it. Levels of acceptance and personal views will vary greatly.
>
> Since Michael was the reason for the training, it may have been beneficial to approach him first and identify his behavior as inappropriate.

2. Michael's version of diversity training was counterproductive and offensive to employees. Was this his intention? Did he do anything right? What did he do wrong?

> Michael felt that he could deliver a "better" diversity training. His intentions did not appear malicious. He made the diversity training into a game, which may have been a helpful way to engage participants. Students should identify that he relied on stereotypes to educate the group, which are often inaccurate and offensive to members of the group. Michael did not create a safe environment to discuss diversity. Since he did not understand why his actions

were inappropriate and warranted the diversity training in the first place, he was not in a position to correct the problems that he had created.

3. How would you create diversity training that is effective and a positive experience for all participants? Is it possible to achieve this?

The goal of diversity training is not to make all employees share the same opinions and beliefs, but rather to acknowledge that differences exist and accommodate the differences in a way that creates a better work environment. Regardless of their differences, everyone in the work environment should feel safe and valued. Diversity training can establish a clear understanding of what is and is not appropriate in a healthy work environment.

There is no way to ensure that any training mechanism will benefit everyone involved because every employee may respond differently to a sensitive topic, particularly if the appropriate behavior proposed requires difficult changes.

ROBERT G. DELCAMPO, PH.D., KRISTIE M. BOUDWIN and SHERRI L. HINES

THE OFFICE
SEASON ONE

Episode 3 – Health Care

Summary: Dunder Mifflin assigns Michael the task of choosing a more cost-effective insurance plan for the office. Michael chooses the most expensive plan, and Jan makes it clear that the goal is to cut costs. Michael does not want to upset the staff and assigns the responsibility to Dwight. Dwight takes his new power to great heights and succeeds in offending staff members and violates the ADA by requesting medical information.

Topics: Motivation, Work-Life Balance, Morale, Job Satisfaction, Extra-Role Behavior, OCB, Psychological Contracts, Employee Benefits

"THAT'S WHAT SHE SAID!"

Clip Description	Start/Stop
"Managers have to pass on bad news—it's part of the job." Michael is charged with selecting a new health care package and delegates the responsibility.	1:20 – 5:13
Dwight has chosen a horrible health plan, and Michael is forced to talk to the employees about the plan. Dwight is enjoying the power.	5:14 – 9:32
In an effort to choose a better health plan for the office, Dwight violates provisions of HIPAA confidentiality and privacy rules, ADA protections, and FMLA by asking employees to write down any diseases they may have so they will be covered under the plan.	9:53 – 10:29
The employees fill out Dwight's form with fictitious diseases. Dwight interviews all employees privately, and Jim locks him in the temporary workspace.	12:53 – 16:10
All employees meet in the conference room, and Dwight continues to gather medical information illegally.	17:15 – 18:50

NOTES:
HIPAA - Health Insurance Portability and Accountability Act of 1996
The HIPAA Privacy Rules restrict the use or disclosure of PHI (protected health information) in individually identifiable health information.

ROBERT G. DELCAMPO, PH.D., KRISTIE M. BOUDWIN and SHERRI L. HINES

Questions for Discussion:

1. Michael has delegated the task of choosing a health insurance plan to Dwight. Is this an appropriate type of task to delegate? If so is there a better choice of employee to delegate this task to? What are the ramifications of this delegation decision?

    In delegating this task to Dwight, Michael has stripped himself of any power in this situation. Although he has also shifted any blame for the negative consequences of selecting a poor health plan, he has more than likely diminished the esteem held for him by the branch employees. Students will perhaps mention that this decision should have been made by Toby, the HR representative in the Scranton office; however it seems more likely that a decision like this would be made on a corporate level with little to no input from the individual branches (although this is not an ideal strategy, in reality decisions are made in this manner routinely).

2. At first, Michael wants to select the premium health plan with maximum benefits but based on fiscal constraints is not allowed to do so. What would you do in this situation? How would you justify the choice of the least expensive health care plan?

    Again, answers here will vary, however it is important to note that in reality tough decisions like this must be made. Michael could have chosen the more expensive plan; however then financial constraints may have forced him to reduce his staff, therein increasing workload and fear of layoffs. It is important to discuss the value of each choice and the trade-offs that must be made in these situations.

3. Dwight asks each employee to give him a detailed description of their medical histories. While we know that this is neither legal nor ethical, what would be the advantage to obtaining this information? Would that be a reasonable benefit for the company? What if companies like Dunder Mifflin asked about risky behaviors such as promiscuity, heavy drinking and smoking?

Most certainly there will be varied opinions on this question too. Some students may note that several private companies have now started to disallow smoking by their employees at any time. It is important to point out in the discussion that the balance of civil liberties in concert with looking out for the best interest of the company is a delicate balance that needs to be maintained.

THE OFFICE
SEASON ONE

Episode 4 – The Alliance

Summary: Morale is low so Michael decides to plan a birthday party for Meredith whose birthday is the closest available. Michael wants to come up with the funniest saying for the card. The downsizing rumors continue so Dwight attempts to form a strategic alliance with John. Oscar solicits donations for a nephew with cerebral palsy participating in a walkathon.

Topics: Downsizing, Appropriate Workplace Behavior, Gender Issues

Clip Description	Start/Stop
Michael harasses Pam for a lack of enthusiasm regarding the party. The women of the office are assigned the task of planning the party. He refers to them as his "party planning beyothches".	2:27 – 5:05
Michael is trying to come up with a witty saying for Meredith's card. Dwight offers a lot of information as well as her personal medical information.	11:02 – 12:01
Michael pledges $25 to Oscar's charity trying to outdo everyone. In this clip Michael "undonates" referring to the "ethics of the thing".	15:10 – 16:40
The reading of the card. Michael offends Meredith with the card and his comments regarding her age and personal history.	17:03 – 20:28

NOTES:

Questions for Discussion:

1. Michael is very keen on the concept of having parties at the office. What are the pros and cons of such a precedent? Do you really think employees are fond of this practice?

    Students will note that sometimes having a party for every birthday, big event, holiday, etc. gets in the way of productivity and can sometimes become a chore. Additionally, when companies celebrate birthdays or "person-specific" holidays, a precedent is set and when it is not followed, certain individuals who are not recognized may become increasingly upset and decrease their level of productivity. Furthermore, some employees truly do come to work just to "work" and their privacy needs to be respected. It should also be noted that certain religions do no approve of "celebrations" for certain events (i.e., birthdays, etc.).

2. Michael donates a significant amount of money at Oscar's request and then attempts to back out of the commitment when he realizes how much money is actually involved. How appropriate is this behavior? How could Michael approach it better? Is it Michael's responsibility as the "boss" to contribute? Is it appropriate to solicit donations at work at all?

    Student opinions will vary in response to these issues and how the situation should have been handled. It should be noted that certain workplaces have policies about solicitation of fellow employees, and it is paramount that employees act in accordance with these policies. If no policy is in place, then the best judgment of the employee should take precedent.

THE OFFICE
SEASON ONE

Episode 5 – Basketball

Summary: Corporate wants employees in the office on Saturday. Michael delegates the unpleasant task of creating the holiday and weekend work schedule to Dwight. The office staff is scheduled to play a basketball game with the warehouse workers. Michael chooses his starting lineup on the basis of stereotypes. Daryl and Michael place a wager on the game—the loser must work on Saturday.

Topics: Team Building, Extra-Role Behavior, Diversity, Stereotypes

Clip Description	Start/Stop
Michael tells the camera about his basketball skills. He delegates the task of creating the weekend schedule to Dwight.	1:19 – 3:10
Michael takes Ryan on a tour of the "whorehouse" and demonstrates how he manages by "walking around." He annoys Darryl and asks Roy if he is still "getting it" from Pam.	3:41 – 4:35
Michael chooses his team and harasses Dwight with name calling. He chooses Stanley "of course," and Stanley calls him on the comment. This segment includes Michael asking Pam to be a cheerleader and wear a skimpy outfit.	5:50 – 9:14
Stanley "the secret weapon" shows up for the game. Once it begins, Michael is disappointed in Stanley's lack of playing ability. He assigns players to guards and notes that Roy is their best player, "Not Lonnie".	11:46 – 13:28
Basketball is like jazz. Michael calls the team together and tells them they are "playing like a bunch of girls". The women are unimpressed.	16:11 – 16:57

NOTES:

"THAT'S WHAT SHE SAID!"

Questions for Discussion:

1. Michael does many things "wrong" in organizing the basketball tournament for the branch, however he also does some things that are positive. What do you think he does that is "good" for the branch?

    Students will note that Michael is attempting to build some level of team cohesion by developing an activity that forces them to participate for a shared goal/cause. Additionally, Michael does attempt to give everyone a role to play in the activity, (although they are assigned stereotypically), in an attempt to get everyone involved.

2. Michael makes a multitude of judgments based on stereotypes in this particular episode. How has this limited his likelihood for success in the basketball tournament? Does this happen in other areas where managers make stereotypical judgments and then somehow limit the opportunity to be successful?

    Answers will vary, however it should be noted that the difficulty with employing stereotypes is that they limit one's view of the abilities and skills that a person might have. In this case Michael judged men and certain minorities as "good basketball players" based on their physical appearance; whereas in reality, the best team in terms of performance would have included some less likely characters.

ROBERT G. DELCAMPO, PH.D., KRISTIE M. BOUDWIN and SHERRI L. HINES

THE OFFICE
SEASON ONE

Episode 6 – Hot Girl

Summary: The Company has created an incentive program to increase sales involving a prize worth $1,000. Pam advises Michael that a woman is at the office selling purses. Michael does not allow the woman to stay until he sees her. All of the men in the office are smitten and try to get her attention. Pam is jealous of the attention given to the woman by the men, especially her fiancé Roy. Katie ends up accepting a ride from Jim.

Topics: Extra-Role Behavior, Motivation, Incentives, Employee Reward Systems, Office Romance

Clip Description	**Start/Stop**
This clip includes inappropriate sexual comments and leering directed to Katie the vendor. Michael compares her to Pam—an upgraded version of Pam.	1:54 – 3:27
Kevin asks Pam if she is jealous because there is another girl in the office and notes that "she is prettier than you".	5:15 – 5:36
Michael introduces Katie to Toby and reveals intimate personal details about Toby's divorce. Michael does not allow office romances.	6:55 – 7:50
Michael asks Pam how girls her age feel about futons. Inappropriate behavior on the part of Pam and Roy in the office make Jim very uncomfortable.	15:25 – 16:25
The employees of Dunder Mifflin are Michael's "special someone." He still knows their names in the morning.	21:31 – 21:55

NOTES:

Questions for Discussion:

1. Michael tells Katie ("The Hot Girl") that he does not allow office romances yet uses his position in the office to woo her. In other episodes, Michael has various liaisons with Jan. How does Michael's double standard about office romance impact his credibility as a leader?

   > Michael makes a blanket statement about office romance that he is not in a position to implement. It has been documented that there is a corporate policy that compels the parties in an office romantic relationship to disclose such information. Additionally, but not adhering to his own "rules," Michael severely damages the level of credibility he has with his employees. Why should they adhere to such mandates if their boss is not setting the proper example? Finally, Katie is not an employee in the Scranton office and thus "office romance" would not be an issue other than the fact that Michael is making advances toward her IN the office. It should also be noted that unwanted advances such as this toward a non-employee can also be considered sexual harassment even though one of the parties, (in this case Katie), are not employed by Dunder Mifflin.

2. In this episode Michael introduces an incentive program for the sales staff that includes a prize of $1,000. Although he may not be able to deliver the prize based on a lack of resources, Michael goes ahead and announces the program. What are the problems with such an announcement? Alternatively what are some more cost effective measures that might motivate the staff to perform? Are these as effective as monetary rewards? To what management theory does Michael subscribe (X or Y) in dealing with his employees? How might this be a problem?

Michael again is damaging his credibility in offering an incentive program that might not ever "pay off". Expectancy theory notes that the relationship between performance and obtaining rewards must be intact to effectively motivate, so in this case if he is unable to reward the high performer with the promised reward, future incentives may also fail as there is a lack of trust in the organization to reward employees as promised. There are many alternative rewards that may be discussed including additional "free" vacation time, flex time scheduling, reduction in future workload, reduction in amount of administrative work or reduction in amount of supervision among other options. The efficacy of these rewards will vary as will student opinions about their efficacy; however it should be noted that monetary rewards are not always the best method to motivate employees. Michael very clearly subscribes to "Theory X" in that he believes his employees are lazy and need to be compelled to work. This could prove problematic when he encounters individuals who are more "Theory Y" and actually enjoy work and require different methods of motivation.

SEASON 2

ROBERT G. DELCAMPO, PH.D., KRISTIE M. BOUDWIN and SHERRI L. HINES

THE OFFICE
SEASON TWO

Episode 2–1 The Dundies

Summary: Corporate does not support the annual employee award ceremony (The Dundies). The budget only allows for one party per year, and Michael's office has already had a number of events. Dwight is upset about comments written on the ladies' bathroom wall. The ceremony at Chili's is filled with inappropriate titles for awards and offensive stereotypical behavior demonstrated by Michael and his variety of characters in his one man show.

Topics: Employee Recognition, Diversity, Appropriate Workplace Behavior, Motivation, Team Building, Job Satisfaction, Morale

Clip Description	Start/Stop
This clip includes the "World's Longest Engagement" award given to Pam. Michael thinks it gets funnier every year. Dwight threatens to take away the ladies bathroom due to the comments written in the stall. Michael gives a pep talk about the Dundies and invites family and friends.	6:21 – 8:36
The Dundies show at Chili's includes Michael offending Stanley and his wife. Michael tells inappropriate jokes and gives out offensive awards. Pam starts drinking a lot.	9:32 – 12:15
The "Hottest in the Office" award goes to a very uncomfortable Ryan. The "Tight-ass" award goes to Angela who refuses to get her award. The "Spicy Curry" award goes to Kelly Kapur who wants to know what the award means.	12:17 – 14:01
The clip includes Michael getting harassed by other patrons in the office. Kevin gets the "Don't Go In There After Me" award. Stanley receives the "Fine Work" award.	14:02 – 16:24

NOTES:

ROBERT G. DELCAMPO, PH.D., KRISTIE M. BOUDWIN and SHERRI L. HINES

Questions for Discussion:

1. Obviously, "The Dundies" are not the most effective form of employee recognition. However, Michael does do some things correctly in attempting to make his employees feel valued. What does he do well? How could "The Dundies" be improved?

    Student responses will vary; however you will note that Michael has attempted to bond the office together in spite of the corporate attempts to not recognize individual employee effort. In this way Michael is attempting to create a bond with his direct reports by going out of his way to create a recognition program that he believes they will appreciate. While Michael has tried to make "The Dundies" enjoyable, he misses the mark a bit by creating awards that are meant to be humorous but become somewhat hurtful. He prays on stereotypes and limited information about the personal lives of each employee rather than rewarding them for a particular facet of their job that they do well.

2. Think about a situation where you were "forced" to attend an event similar to "The Dundies" (this could be at work or school). Why did you attend? Did it end up being "fun"? Why do companies attempt to place their employees in social situations with the goal of making them more comfortable at work? Is this ever effective?

    Once again, student responses will vary; however students will probably note that it is regularly assumed that organizations believe their employees would like to have social gatherings that no one seems personally drawn to. Bring up the concept that the purpose served by close, social, personal relationships is a "double-edged sword" of sorts. While it will create embeddedness (a key predictor of employee turnover) and "links" to the organization, it can also hinder the day-to-day operation of the company in that it may be difficult for individuals to talk openly to each other about their work performance, etc.

3. It appears that Michael is attempting to motivate his employees by employing the expectancy theory of motivation. How has he erred in applying this model?

Expectancy Theory rests on the concept that employees understand the relationship between their effort-to-performance, self-efficacy in achieving levels of performance, the fact that performance will result in reward and that rewards are tied to their personal goals. In this instance Michael believes that the Dunder Mifflin employees are not only interested in receiving a "Dundie," (reward fitting with personal goals), but also that their performance has something to do with receiving a "Dundie". Being in touch with the needs and wants of one's employees is key in this situation, and obviously Michael is far out of touch with their preferences for being rewarded.

4. The Dunder Mifflin-Scranton employees are all very heavily involved and informed about each other's lives away from work. What are the benefits to such close ties? What are the problems that it poses in their everyday functioning? Is there an ideal level of rapport that employees/managers, etc. should have?

In this case students will have many different types of responses. This sort of question is more to stimulate discussion around the pros and cons of creating a cohesive work force. While the organization's culture will be strong, it is necessary to note that it will also be difficult to change; and depending on the goals and strategy of the organization, different levels of cohesion might be preferred.

ROBERT G. DELCAMPO, PH.D., KRISTIE M. BOUDWIN and SHERRI L. HINES

THE OFFICE
SEASON TWO

Episode 2–2 Sexual Harassment

Corporate is cracking down on sexual harassment in the office. Michael's friend Todd Packer visits the office, and he is filled with obscene jokes and inoffensive behavior. Pam is worried about her mother coming to visit the office because of the offensive behavior.

Topics: Sexual Harassment, Communication, Electronic Monitoring, Training

Clip Description	Start/Stop
Michael describes himself as the "King of Forwards." He likes to joke around and forward inappropriate emails, i.e. "50 Signs Your Priest May Be Michael Jackson."	0:32 – 3:38
Michael requests the monkey sex link so he can forward it "like it's hot." Toby will be providing a review of the company's sexual harassment policy to all staff.	4:43 – 6:49
Policy review—Pam is concerned because her mother is coming for a visit, and she usually gets sexually harassed on sexual harassment training day. Michael brings a blowup doll to the meeting. Michael wants Pam to act out a lesbian situation with the blowup doll.	8:12 - 11:13
The men are watching the HR video when Daryl recognizes the actress in the video. Michael announces to the office that Daryl "banged" the girl in the video—just in time for Jan and the corporate	12:43 – 13:51

"THAT'S WHAT SHE SAID!"

lawyer to hear.	
Packer returns spouting obscene statements and profanity. Michael is upset that he can't" say anything" to anyone anymore. He announces that he can no longer be friends with the people in the office and that he is retiring from comedy.	13:52 – 16:44
Packer tells an obscene joke at Elizabeth's expense. Michael points out that Kevin's behavior crossed the line and sends Kevin to his desk.	18:50 – 21:03
NOTES:	

Questions for Discussion:

1. Michael mentions his self-appointed title "King of Forwards"; what are the problems with allowing employees to use corporate e-mail for personal use? What might be an alternative arrangement?

   Students may discuss the "freedom" of using corporate e-mail/internet as well as the perception of its use as an additional benefit provided by the company. While valid, it is important to bring up the concept that if an employer is paying for 40 hours of work per week, they expect to receive 40 full hours of work per week. Bandwidth, opening the company to harassment issues and wear and tear on equipment might be brought up as issues to counter the personal use of e-mail/internet. While no solution is perfect, it is important for students to understand the potential issues posed.

2. Sexual Harassment is a growing issue in the corporate sector; what are the specific instances of both quid pro quo ("something for something") and hostile environment that are demonstrated in this episode. How would you design a training program to address these issues?

   The number of instances in this episode is limitless. It is important to note however that some of the quid pro quo instances can also create hostile environment situations. Just because an individual is not the direct target of quid pro quo harassment does not mean that the situation is not harassing. The individual can feel uncomfortable based on the situation created by the quid pro quo proposal. It should also be noted that hostile environment lawsuits are more difficult to prosecute.

3. Some employees (Michael, Packer, etc.) are sometimes unreceptive to training such as sexual harassment training. How should this type of employee be dealt with? While it is easy to suggest that they just be dismissed, is this really the best option? What other options might be explored before moving to this level?

Many students jump immediately to firing the offending or perceived to be offending employee. While this is in some cases necessary, it is essential to note that the company itself is liable for providing training to these individuals to the best of their ability. Perhaps different methods are more effective for different individuals. In this case the typical "seminar" method seems to not "take" with employees like Michael and Packer. For this type of individual, perhaps one on one counseling or more information of how this sort of behavior negatively impacts productivity would improve their understanding of the issues at hand. Additionally, it should be noted that if proper documentation is not kept, there is potential for unfair dismissal claims to be made.

ROBERT G. DELCAMPO, PH.D., KRISTIE M. BOUDWIN and SHERRI L. HINES

THE OFFICE
SEASON TWO

Episode 2–3 Office Olympics

Summary: Michael and Dwight are out of the office for the day to close on Michael's condo. Jim discovers that Oscar and Kevin play a made-up game called "Hateball" that leads him to discover Toby made up a game called Dunderball. At this point, Jim decides that the day should be devoted to Office Olympics. He and Pam organize what turns out to be a very festive and morale boosting day—even to Michael and Dwight who have no idea what is happening.

Topics: Job Descriptions, Motivation, Work-Life Balance, Team Building, Morale, Job Satisfaction, Extra-Role Behavior, OCB, Psychological Contracts

"THAT'S WHAT SHE SAID!"

Clip Description	Start/Stop
Michael and Ryan are at the office very very early. Ryan realizes that the only reason he is in at that hour is to deliver Michael's breakfast sandwich. Michael makes an inappropriate comment about Ryan removing his pants.	0:00 – 0:49
This clip includes Michael speaking offensively but states that it is not offensive because "they talk like that in the movies." Michael questions Pam about changing his personal magazine subscriptions.	3:33 – 4:21
Oscar and Kevin play a paper football game called "Hate Ball" when Michael is out of the office or when they are bored. Jim plays a game. It is called Hate Ball because Angela hates it.	4:52 – 5:46
Dwight asks numerous questions. The real estate agent and association president mistake Michael and Dwight for a gay couple.	6:22 – 7:38
Michael and Dwight return to the office in time for the last lap of "don't spill the coffee." Everyone returns to their desk and the office returns to normal. Jim and Pam conduct closing ceremonies including Michael and Dwight. Michael is moved to tears.	16:52 – 20:57
NOTES: This episode could be broken down to support team building and morale.	

ROBERT G. DELCAMPO, PH.D., KRISTIE M. BOUDWIN and SHERRI L. HINES

Questions for Discussion

1. Michael has created an environment in which his employees are uncertain as to how "far" their job descriptions go. What are the potential problems with this sort of arrangement (i.e., Ryan bringing the breakfast sandwich, Pam changing magazine subscriptions, etc.)? What recourse do the employees have in this situation if they are uncomfortable performing such tasks? What would you do in a similar situation?

    This is an interesting discussion to have with students when covering job descriptions. This sort of dilemma occurs many times for "entry level" workers. For example, you have a good job that you are happy to have but your boss expects you to get them coffee every morning...what do you do? Or alternatively, on the first day your boss asks for a cup of coffee, you get it, you have now set up the expectation that this is something you will do...how dangerous is this? Thought provoking discussion on these issues should develop from these types of questions. While there is no one particular answer that fits these questions, it is important to think about the extra-role behaviors that individuals deem acceptable.

2. The Office Olympics may be viewed as a waste of time or to infringe on productivity, but what are the positive outcomes of such activities? Is it possible that unexpected, fun, breaks could actually increase later productivity and in turn provide a great return on investment? Where do we draw the line? Why are so many office "fun" activities sometimes dreaded by employees?

    Students will undoubtedly respond that they find it essential to have both a fun and rewarding job in which they are productive. In this discussion it is essential to focus on realistic expectations of how to balance a "fun" workplace and a productive workplace. Instructors may focus on the concepts of autonomy, task variety, skill variety, etc. in order to make the actual tasks of one's job more rewarding and fun. While it is essential to have a committed, bonded group of workers, it is important to focus on how to achieve this without offending or infringing on other's needs to be productive and professional in the workplace.

3. At the end of the episode Michael is moved to tears by the bonding that has occurred in the office through the day's events. There are many similar instances throughout the series in which Michael stresses his interest in bonding with the employees and bonding them together as a team. Is this really a good idea? What level of emotional involvement from management is necessary to have a functioning work unit?

Responses will vary to these questions; however it should be noted that depending on the type of work being done, supervisors may be more or less emotionally involved. This is especially the case in non-profit organizations—i.e., perhaps the supervisor is particularly committed to the cause, etc.—which can pose issues when employees treat the experience as "just a job," wherein the differing opinions can cause strife.

ROBERT G. DELCAMPO, PH.D., KRISTIE M. BOUDWIN and SHERRI L. HINES

THE OFFICE
SEASON TWO

Episode 2–4 The Fire

Summary: A fire in the kitchen forces everyone out of the office into the parking lot. To pass the time, Jim suggests they play games. Michael discovers that Ryan is going to business school and decides to act as mentor. Dwight becomes very jealous and feels left out. He returns to the building to look for Michael's cell phone. Dwight informs the staff that Ryan started the fire and labels him "Fire Guy."

Topics: Workplace Safety and Health, Communication, Appropriate Workplace Behavior, Mentoring, Gender Issues, Equal Opportunity

"THAT'S WHAT SHE SAID!"

Clip Description	Start/Stop
The fire alarm goes off. Angela and Dwight work to clear the office while Michael makes a run for the door. He explains that women and children should go first but Dunder Mifflin does not employ children and women are equal—by law.	3:31 – 5:18
Jim suggests games for the employees to play in the parking lot. The games are Desert Island, Who Would you Do, and Would You Rather.	6:23 – 8:09
Michael checks out Ryan's car and notices the business books. He begins calling him "Egg Head" and pinches Ryan's nipples. Ryan quizzes Michael on business. Dwight gets overly physical with Ryan.	9:18 – 11:30
The game of "Who Would You Do?" begins. Roy would do "the tightass Christian chick"; Jim would do Kevin; Michael would have sex with Ryan; Roy proclaims they are all gay.	14:49 – 16:17
NOTES:	

ROBERT G. DELCAMPO, PH.D., KRISTIE M. BOUDWIN and SHERRI L. HINES

Questions for Discussion

1. Michael refers to the concept that women are "equal—by law" as rationale for him leaving the building first. What are the implications of societal assumptions such as "women and children first"? Does this hinder women in the workplace? What are some other gender stereotypes that are difficult to break down? While this is presented in a somewhat humorous fashion how do we balance these perceived "courtesies" with attempts to create equality in the workplace?

    Students will have varied opinions on these topics. While they are potentially flash-point issues, it is important to discuss true feelings about these topics. It is also useful to bring up the concept of "suppressing" certain feelings at work. If someone has a misogynistic attitude, how should they act at work? Should an organization employ this person? How should they be managed?

2. Angela and Dwight take the initiative to maintain order when vacating the office. What procedures should be in place for the workplace to maintain its level of safety? How specific should these policies be?

    It is important to note that specific policies will vary from workplace to workplace, but basic fire safety is of the utmost importance. Proper training is required in these areas to limit liability for the company too.

3. During the game of "Who would you do?" Roy proclaims that everyone is "gay". In reality, homosexuality is one of the most common facets of diversity that is commonly overlooked or treated as "ok" to make fun of, what are the potential problems with these assumptions? How prevalent are these assumptions in the American workplace? What sort of programs could be

implemented to bring these to the forefront? Are diversity sensitivity programs that might be used truly effective? Can people's deeply held opinions really be changed?

> *The pervasiveness of homosexual stereotypes are some of the most common in today's society. A quick view of primetime television or popular movies will elucidate these stereotypes. The acceptance of homosexuality is also a flashpoint issue as religious, political and traditional values come into play. In this case it is paramount to preach tolerance and understanding of alternative lifestyles. While the ultimate goal would be acceptance, it is important for all viewpoints, liberal and conservative, to be at least heard and respected no matter how divergent. It is however, unacceptable for anyone to use offensive, hurtful or derogatory language in this discussion.*

ROBERT G. DELCAMPO, PH.D., KRISTIE M. BOUDWIN and SHERRI L. HINES

THE OFFICE
SEASON TWO

Episode 2–5 Halloween

Summary: The employees are dressed up celebrating Halloween. Michael is upset and stressed out because downsizing has become a reality. He was supposed to have fired one of his employees and has until the end of the day to make a decision. He has no idea who to fire and consults with Dwight. Eventually Michael chooses Creed, but Creed talks him out of it and suggests Devon be fired. Devon does not take the news well and smashes a pumpkin on Michael's car. Jim and Pam post Dwight's resume on job search websites.

Topics: Downsizing, Job Security, Job Satisfaction, Team Building and Morale, Employee Termination, Managerial Decision Making

"THAT'S WHAT SHE SAID!"

Clip Description	**Start/Stop**
Michael roams the office making offensive comments to Oscar and Kim about their costumes. Oscar is dressed as a woman, and Kim is dressed as Dorothy from Oz. Michael suggests that she dress like the girl in Bend It Like Beckham.	4:12 – 5:40
Michael calls Dwight in to help him decide who to fire. Michael thinks that firing the least popular would have the least affect on morale. Dwight and his "extra head" have a conversation about firing Dwight.	6:46 – 7:45
Dwight was given the task of firing Stanley. He attempts to fire Stanley, but Stanley merely laughs. Dwight lets Michael know that Stanley would not listen to him, and that he will have to fire Stanley himself.	9:22 – 10:14
Michael asks Jim to role play firing Michael to help him prepare. Jim mocks him and gets thrown out of the office. Michael tries to fire Creed, but Creed talks Michael into firing Devon.	14:05 – 19:53
NOTES:	

Questions for Discussion

1. Downsizing is a reality for many organizations. Using the difficulty faced by Michael in this particular episode, how should decisions about "who to downsize" be made? How does organized (union) labor change this decision making process?

    In this discussion it is important to discuss what criteria are reasonable to use for a basis to lay off employees. Some defensible types will include performance, tenure, level in the organization, job centrality and others. The concept of job sharing may arise which is also a good solution. When unions enter the picture, there are normally very specific guidelines for layoffs that can only occur in certain situations. The criteria used are normally tenure-based when dealing with organized labor.

2. Michael attempts to role play to prepare himself to fire Creed. His strategies do not work, and he is convinced to fire Devon. How would such indecisiveness impact a manager like Michael in the workplace? How could he regain credibility after such a quick change of heart?

    Michael is more than likely viewed by his employees as somewhat of a "push over". This is evidenced by many of his employees trying to sway his opinion on who to lay off. While at the outset it appears that this is a negative characteristic, properly managed, someone who accepts input from his employees in making decisions is actually an outstanding manager. The key is where to draw the line in allowing communication.

3. How effective is Michael in his decision to fire Devon? What did he do correctly? What did he do incorrectly? How could his decision making process be improved?

> *Michael has taken input from many employees, which is good. He has also attempted to use some sort of criteria in determining who to lay off; however he does not stick to his initial decision of who should be fired, diminishing his credibility in future situations. Michael could have evaluated his alternatives and their ramifications before putting his plan into action. The application of some text-based decision making models would also be useful.*

4. When Michael decides to fire Stanley he delegates the task to Dwight. Dwight is unable to complete the task. Is this the sort of task that Michael should delegate? Why or why not? How could he have handled it differently? Would the outcome be different?

> *Michael tries desperately throughout the series to assert himself as a leader; however when difficult tasks occur he is continually unable to complete them. A true leader is able to do both the attractive and unattractive demands of his/her job. Additionally, Michael has delegated the task of firing Stanley to Dwight who has limited credibility within the office. Dwight not only has diminished position power, but he also lacks referent power in that his peers do not take him seriously.*

ROBERT G. DELCAMPO, PH.D., KRISTIE M. BOUDWIN and SHERRI L. HINES

THE OFFICE
SEASON TWO

Episode 2–6 The Fight

Summary: Once every year, the staff experiences the "perfect storm"—all of Michael's work overlaps causing people to work late. Michael gets physical with Dwight and, in an effort to demonstrate how "tough" he is, Michael takes an embarrassing punch to the stomach from Dwight. Jim and Pam engineer a rematch to be held at Dwight's dojo during lunch. The two have an awkward encounter at the dojo.

Topics: Managing Work Flows, Appropriate Work-Place Behavior, Office Romance

"THAT'S WHAT SHE SAID!"

Clip Description	Start/Stop
Dwight's desk and belongings have been moved into the restroom.	0:00 – 1:35
Dwight and Jim discuss the various employees that Dwight could beat up. Michael grabs Dwight and puts him into a sleeper hold. To demonstrate his toughness, Michael takes a punch to the stomach that almost knocks him down.	7:44 – 10:22
Jim engineers a rematch between Dwight and Michael. Michael and Dwight exchange words and decide to fight at the dojo. The entire office goes to the dojo to watch the fight.	10:42 – 13:29
At the dojo, Jim and Pam flirt. Pam gets upset when Jim picks her up and others notice. Jim is confused by her response to their flirting.	13:32 – 14:12

NOTES:

Questions for Discussion:

1. At the beginning of the episode we see that Jim has once again played a prank on Dwight, moving all of his materials in the office restroom. While this is obviously for comedic purposes, in a typical office how "far" should someone take a prank? It is never "ok" to pull a prank? How should one manage their impression in the workplace in regard to "pulling pranks"?

    Responses will differ here, but what is important is the balance between keeping the workplace fun and keeping the workplace safe. It is a fine line to walk.

2. If Dwight had been pranked in this way in a typical work place, and he was upset, what is the best way for him to respond? Who should he confront? What are the potential issues caused by confronting the "pranker"? By confronting his boss?

    Most companies will have formal procedures in place for complaints against management and co-workers, however just as in many interpersonal relationships perhaps it is best to personally confront the individual before entering into some formal disciplinary procedure. Of course depending on the severity of the event, the response should be measured.

3. Jim and Pam have an underlying office romance that is brought up many times in several episodes. In this particular episode Jim makes Pam uncomfortable by picking her up. Is this sexual harassment? How do you know that it is/isn't? If someone is romantically interested in another person in the office, (mutual admiration or not), how should they proceed?

    This again is a tricky question to answer. While a high percentage of long-term relationships emerge from the workplace it is increasingly difficult to act on personal feelings at work. This is why discussion of these topics is paramount. The discussion demonstrates the level to which different individuals are comfortable with different levels/types of interaction.

4. Some companies forbid office romances; why do you think this is the case? Is this a good idea? What are the issues created by implementing such a policy? What liability issues are created when there is not such a policy?

See above. Many of the same issues but spun a bit differently.

THE OFFICE
SEASON TWO

Episode 2–7 The Client

Summary: Jan and Michael meet with an important potential client at Chili's. Michael eventually impresses Jan with his ability to woo and eventually win the client. The meeting lasts all day and involves drinking. After the meeting, Jan and Michael spend time together. Back at the office, Pam finds Michael's screenplay and the office staff do a reading. After work, Pam and Jim share a sandwich and watch Dwight's fireworks display.

Topics: Communication, Office Romance, Workplace Privacy, Peter Principle

"THAT'S WHAT SHE SAID!"

Clip Description	Start/Stop
Michael and Jan are leaving for a big meeting with a representative from the County. Michael was going to shut down the office—because "they don't get very much work done when I'm not here."	3:04 – 4:02
The parties meet at Chili's and during introductions, Michael discovers that Jan has been divorced. Michael takes over the meeting with an Awesome Blossom. Pam limits him to one joke, so he calls Pam who reads through his various joke books to find an appropriate joke.	4:42 – 6:42
While putting the joke books away, Pam discovers a screenplay in Michael's desk and shares it with Jim.	6:43 – 7:31
Jim and the employees prepare to do a reading of the screenplay. Dwight accuses them of taking it and copying it. Once Jim offers Dwight the lead role, he is no longer upset.	8:01 – 8:32
Jan and Michael celebrate sealing the deal. The next morning, Dwight sees Jan arrive by cab and figures out that she and Michael spent the night together. Michael arrives and talks about the evening. Jan calls and tells him the evening was a mistake and accuses him of drugging her or getting her drunk.	14:59 – 19:53
NOTES:	

Questions for Discussion

1. Michael has his privacy breeched in a few ways in this particular episode. In what ways has his privacy been breeched? Is this acceptable?

    Michael's privacy has been breached in that the office is buzzing about his rumored encounter with Jan, as well as Pam disclosing his personal property (screenplay). Rationale will differ but more than likely surround the concepts of Michael leaving his personal property at work and self-disclosing his encounter with Jan.

2. Jan has some level of disdain for Michael's ideas about how to complete the sales meeting. Ultimately, Michael is able to complete the deal. Was Jan justified in questioning Michael's tactics? While somewhat inappropriate, should Michael be penalized for using questionable tactics?

    Michael has some unorthodox tactics without question. However, he is able to complete his job. Being able to "read" people and situations for appropriate behavior is one of the most important but difficult to teach skills necessary for success. Perhaps Michael's ability to understand the dynamics of a sales situation should be harnessed somehow and "toned down" based on corporate policy.

3. The extent of Michael and Jan's liaison is unknown at this point. Earlier we discussed office romances, how do the dynamics of this situation change when it is between a boss and an employee? How would this situation be different if Michael were a woman and Jan a man?

Gender issues such as these can cause some tricky discussion. It is important to note however that when the roles are reversed that there is a much different reaction to how the situation should be handled. This illuminates the fact that while gender stereotypes are breaking down in some areas, they still thrive in others. At this point it is interesting to have a discussion of where and why certain gender stereotypes exist.

4. Michael is obviously a skilled salesperson. It seems that his sales acuity is the reason he was promoted to Regional Manager. How often does this happen (someone who is good at one task is then converted into management)? Is this a good tactic? If these individuals have no formal management training or expertise, why are they promoted?

   This is an ideal place to discuss the "Peter Principle", which is that people "rise to their level of incompetence". While it has underlying tones of being an argument for professional management, it is interesting to discuss why people who are good in sales are promoted to management; good front-line managers are promoted to high level corporate directors and so on. While these skill sets are totally orthogonal. they are continually assumed to be somehow related. The discussion of this phenomenon should create some interesting discourse.

ROBERT G. DELCAMPO, PH.D., KRISTIE M. BOUDWIN and SHERRI L. HINES

THE OFFICE
SEASON TWO

Episode 2–8 Performance Review

Summary: Today is company wide performance review. Michael meets with each employee individually and solicits feedback regarding his relationship with Jan. Jan will be conducting his performance review in the afternoon. He really has no ideas to share with Jan so he calls a meeting to go through the employee suggestion box. Dwight believes today is "Friday," and Pam and Jim help perpetuate the belief.

Topics: Performance Appraisal, Job Descriptions, Appropriate Workplace Behavior, Employee Feedback, Communication, Office Romance, Fairness

"THAT'S WHAT SHE SAID!"

Clip Description	**Start/Stop**
Dwight has a new exercise orb and drives Jim crazy telling him about the benefits, including the sexual benefits. When Jim finds out the orb costs $25.00, he stabs it with a pair of scissors.	0:00 – 1:09
Pam's review consists of her interpretation of a voicemail message from Jan. Pam quickly realizes that in order to get a good review, she must provide positive feedback on Michael's relationship with Jan.	1:44 – 4:14
This clip sets out some of the problems with office romances. Jan wants to talk about performance review and Michael's ideas for improving business. Michael believes the meeting is about what happened between them.	6:30 – 8:11
Jan arrives for Michael's performance review. Michael gets a little too physical and makes an inappropriate comment. Jan tries to keep discussions limited to company business.	9:35 – 12:26
Jan attends the office suggestion box meeting. Michael has not looked at the box in several years. There are suggestions referring to Michael's body odor and coffee breath. Also, a suggestion to "not sleep with your boss."	12:28 – 15:44
Michael follows Jan out of the office asking why there is no relationship. Jan finally tells him the hard truth.	18:49 – 20:27
NOTES:	

Questions for Discussion

1. Michael conducts many "performance appraisals" in this particular episode. What specifically does he do incorrectly? Does he do anything correctly? How could he do a better job?

    Michael is performing the performance appraisals only because he is compelled to do so by corporate. There is no prescribed format or objective. Specifically, Michael could do collaborative goal setting, management by objectives, etc. However, he does do some things correctly. Michael does meet one-on-one with each employee, he tries to develop a relationship with each and acts as an advocate for each employee.

2. In this episode we see some specific examples of the problems created by office romances, in this case with Jan and Michael. Are these realistic? How could this sort of relationship further complicate normal forms of interaction such as a performance appraisal?

    These types of problems are quite realistic. It is difficult when power differences exist in the work place and then reflect in a personal relationship too. For this reason many companies (including Dunder Mifflin as we find out later in the series) require a declaration of the existence of a consensual relationship so that any official interaction between the two parties can be properly monitored.

3. Imagine that Michael and Jan are truly in a relationship at this point. How would the performance appraisal take place? How would Dunder Mifflin be able to monitor a situation such as this? Can this sort of situation result in a "fair" appraisal? What might be some problems with the outcome?

> *In this case Dunder Mifflin would either appoint an HR representative to be present during the appraisal to insure fairness or the appraisal would be performed by Jan's superior. Written documentation would be necessary to make note of the intricacies of the event in the employee's personnel file.*

4. Dunder Mifflin-Scranton has implemented an office "suggestion box" to try and improve their office functioning. Is this a good way for an office such as this to bring to light potentially offensive behavior/situations they are unhappy with? What are your reactions to the way Michael handles the suggestion box meeting? Should these complaints be handled more privately? Why/Why not? What might be a better way to get the same information in a more constructive way?

> *The suggestion box is a decent idea; however Michael sees it more as problems about "others" rather than problems with him. Michael does not take any of the suggestions seriously (especially those that deal with him) and quickly dismisses them even though they may be of importance to the individual who wrote them. "Suggestions" at the core are more constructive than simple criticism as they lend themselves as ways to improve the situation rather than simply complain. In this case some suggestions might be better implemented in a more private fashion or perhaps with some mediation from an HR representative.*

ROBERT G. DELCAMPO, PH.D., KRISTIE M. BOUDWIN and SHERRI L. HINES

THE OFFICE
SEASON TWO

Episode 2–9 Email Surveillance

Summary: Michael has software installed allowing him to read emails sent out by the staff. IT notifies the staff and they immediately begin deleting items. Pam suspects that Dwight and Angela may have a relationship. While reading employee email, Michael discovers an invitation to a barbeque at Jim's house. He also discovers that he has not been invited. Michael tries unsuccessfully to get an invitation and attends an improvisation class. Later, he crashes the party.

Topics: E-Mail Surveillance, Electronic Monitoring, Employee Privacy, Outside of work relationships, Office Romance, Communication

"THAT'S WHAT SHE SAID!"

Clip Description	Start/Stop
Michael freaks out when he sees a man with a turban who turns out to be the IT tech. He locks the door and turns out the lights.	0:00 - 49
Michael is setting up a software program to enable him to read staff email. He performs a search on himself and reads what is being written about him. IT distributed a notice that they were under email surveillance.	2:25 – 4:14
Social relationships. Michael finds an invitation to a BBQ at Jim's house and discovers that he has not been invited. He really wants to get invited to the party.	5:52 – 6:22
This clip includes Michael's philosophy on the distance between a boss and employee. He joins the staff for lunch and tries to wrangle an invitation to the party.	6:50 – 8:21
At 5:05, Michael talks to every single employee leaving for the day asking about their plans. He calls an Angela a "liar" when she reveals her plans.	10:45 – 12:03
NOTES:	

ROBERT G. DELCAMPO, PH.D., KRISTIE M. BOUDWIN and SHERRI L. HINES

Questions for Discussion:

1. Michael has implemented an e-mail monitoring program with little-to-no notification for his employees. What are the potential problems with this program? Can a company do this sort of thing without notifying their employees? Is the use of Michael's time to read employee email a good use of company "resources"? Are there any other forms of email monitoring that might be better?

    Most companies have clauses in their contracts or terms of employment that inform employees that their communication will be monitored. In the case of implementing a new system, even though the company does not need to notify their employees, they would be best served in notifying them of the timing, reasoning and rationale for implementing the program. Open and honest communication is the best policy for implementing any new policy with a company.

2. Jim has invited all of his officemates, save Michael, to his party. Was this a wise move? In terms of impression management and office politics, how might he have handled this situation differently and still not have Michael attend the party? Is that possible?

    This again is a question of opinion; however in terms of impression management, it might have been best to "bite the bullet" and invite Michael to the party. Perhaps he could have presented the party in a different way to make it somewhat unattractive to Michael, therein limiting the possibility that he would attend yet still maintain his esteem in Michael's opinion.

3. Michael interrogates all of his employees toward the end of the day trying to pry their evening plans out. This culminates in Michael talking with Angela and calling her "a liar". What are the

ramifications of such mistrust and prying conversation? Will this impact productivity? Will this impact the possibility of future invitations for Michael to future parties?

Michael has taken the non-invitation to Jim's party very personally. By continually questioning his employees, he is not only hindering daily productivity, but he is also creating a high level of distrust and uneasiness in the workplace. This could harm future outside-of-work functions as few people would be motivated to plan an activity that would be so difficult to manage.

ROBERT G. DELCAMPO, PH.D., KRISTIE M. BOUDWIN and SHERRI L. HINES

THE OFFICE
SEASON TWO

Episode 2–10 Christmas Party

Summary: Michael plans an office holiday party. Names were drawn for gift giving, but Michael changes the gift exchange to a "Yankee Swap." The game allows recipients to exchange their gift for one that has already been opened or a wrapped gift. Michael's gift of an iPod for Ryan exceeds the $20.00 limit and becomes the main focus of Yankee Swap. To brighten the mood and raise morale, Michael makes vodka shots available and the party begins.

Topics: Motivation, Psychological Contracts, Equity Theory, Recognition and Rewards, Appropriate Workplace Behavior

Clip Description	Start/Stop
The clip includes the party planning committee and Michael's inappropriate Christmas time jokes. What he has in mind is a "Playboy Mansion"-type party. Michael refuses to loan Daryl the Santa hat.	2:41 – 4:48
Michael explains that presents show how much you care for someone. Michael bought Ryan a video iPod over the $20 limit. Michael gets really upset over his gift from Phyllis and changes the game to Yankee swap. Everyone but Michael is upset over the change in plans.	6:43 – 10:45
Employees are doing vodka shots, and Packer shows up at the party with mistletoe in his pants. The party gets out of control and physical. Meredith removes her top in an effort to get Michael's attention.	18:40 – 21:16

NOTES:

ROBERT G. DELCAMPO, PH.D., KRISTIE M. BOUDWIN and SHERRI L. HINES

Questions for Discussion

1. Michael purchases an iPod for the Secret Santa exchange, knowing full well that he is above the $20 limit. Although he offers his motivation on camera, what do you think his true motivation for purchasing such an extravagant gift? Why does he become angry?

    Michael has certain expectations about the Secret Santa exchange. When the gift Michael receives does not meet his expectations his psychological contract is violated and negative consequences ensue. This demonstrates that grave consequences can arise upon violation of the psychological contract on a larger scale too (i.e., work agreement, boss-employee relationship, etc.).

2. Michael has certain expectations about what is supposed to happen at the party; how does this mirror the psychological contract that he has somehow created? What are the negative consequences that we see of the violated contract? Reflect on a time where events did not unfold as you planned. What was the outcome in this situation?

    See above. This serves as yet another example of unmet expectations and their consequences.

3. There are many inappropriate events that occur during the office party. What specific events are inappropriate and why? What policies should be put in place to make sure that Dunder Mifflin limits its liability?

    There are many examples of inappropriate behavior in the office. Using company funds to supply alcohol, the urging of other employees to drink, creating unsafe and uncomfortable situations among employees are among these inappropriate events. Dunder Mifflin apparently has some policies to limit their liability, but they are ignored by Michael. This brings up the concept that policies only serve a purpose if they are actually put into action. Further training or penalties for not adhering to policy might be necessary to reinforce their importance.

4. Is the concept of having a Christmas party the best idea? What is the reasoning for having such a party? What might be a more effective celebration/reward in this case?

Once again, the rewards utilized in the Dunder Mifflin-Scranton office do not meet with the values of its employees. While they look forward to the Christmas party, the money and effort put into its planning might be better used in a different fashion. Additionally, having a Christmas party might alienate employees with different religions or belief systems.

ROBERT G. DELCAMPO, PH.D., KRISTIE M. BOUDWIN and SHERRI L. HINES

THE OFFICE
SEASON TWO

Episode 2–11 Booze Cruise

Summary: Michael plans a motivational cruise on a party boat on Lake Wallenpaupack. There are a number of parties not affiliated with Dunder Mifflin, and the party games and contests make it very difficult for Michael to make his presentation. He also encounters problems with Captain Jack. Roy is moved after talking to Captain Jack and announces a wedding date. Jim and Katie break up.

Topics: Motivation, Leadership, Recognition and Rewards, Communication, Teams, Team Building

"THAT'S WHAT SHE SAID!"

Clip Description	**Start/Stop**
Michael has planned a first quarter camaraderie get together—a leadership training exercise on a harbor cruise (booze cruise.) Michael compares the office to a ship, and he is the captain. This is his model of teamwork and he is unable to get the concept across.	1:31 – 6:21
This clip includes a power struggle between the captain and Michael. Michael wants to be the leader.	7:22 – 8:28
Michael decides to go ahead and give the motivational talk. He tries to share his boat analogy with the group and announces that the ship is sinking. A frightened man jumps overboard, and Michael ends up in the brig.	16:56 – 18:27

NOTES:

Questions for Discussion

1. Michael attempts to get his concept of "teamwork" across on the boat. Why is he ineffective in communicating his message? Is his concept realistic? How might he better get this message across?

   Michael has chosen an inappropriate time to try and deliver his message. Under the guise of a "fun" outing, Michael has attempted to insert some of his "management parables" in order to enrich his employees. Once again his expectations are a bit unrealistic, and he is left unfulfilled. While "management parables" might not be learned, such a social gathering of co-workers could still be valuable and should not be discounted.

2. Michael and Captain Jack have a "power struggle". What are the leadership qualities of both Captain Jack and Michael? What are their bases of power? If Captain Jack were to come into the Dunder Mifflin-Scranton office, how would he be received?

   Students will note many differences in Michael and Captain Jack. Each has specific leadership qualities, but it is key to note that these characteristics are not applicable in all settings. If Captain Jack were to walk into the office of Dunder Mifflin-Scranton, he would not be well received if he encouraged employees to limbo and drink. The situation an individual is placed in has just as much impact on their ability to lead as the characteristics they possess.

3. Do you think that Michael could do anything to enhance his credibility as a leader? So overall, are leaders born or made? Does Michael believe he is a leader? Why/why isn't that enough to make him a leader? Does Michael have to be a leader to be an effective branch manager?

Students will have varied opinions on whether leaders are born or made. Rather than having a surface-level discussion, ask them to explore what aspects of leadership are in-born and which can be developed. More likely than not, a solution of "a little of each" will arise, but exploring the issue more deeply is of some use. Certain individuals have characteristics that draw people to them and others simply do not. How does one explain this situation? An interesting discussion of "born or made" can be of the utmost importance when introducing theories of leadership.

ROBERT G. DELCAMPO, PH.D., KRISTIE M. BOUDWIN and SHERRI L. HINES

THE OFFICE
SEASON TWO

Episode 2–12 The Injury

Summary: Michael burns his foot on a George Foreman Grill and is unable to drive. Dwight rushes off to pick him up and gets into a car accident. He has a concussion causing him to act normal and very nice. Michael's requests for assistance go well above and beyond the call of duty, and the staff will not comply with his requests. Dismayed with the staff's lack of care and understanding, Michael conducts a disability meeting.

Topics: Diversity, Communication, ADA, Extra-Role Behavior, OCB

"THAT'S WHAT SHE SAID!"

Clip Description	**Start/Stop**
Michael has injured his foot and the staff is forced to deal with the injury. Michael gives Pam a hard time for not coming to pick him up. Dwight is acting strange.	3:19 – 5:27
This clip shows some of the outrageous requests made by Michael. He calls Pam and asks that she rub butter on his foot and when she declines, he starts yelling for Ryan.	6:36 – 7:07
Michael falls off of the toilet and requests help. Toby and Ryan are in the vicinity but do not assist. Toby advises Michael to get up himself—he only cooked his foot. Michael is very upset because no one understands disability.	8:27 – 11:27
Michael has pinned copies of famous people with disabilities on the wall. He has included Tom Hanks twice—Forest Gump and as the actor from the movie Big. The Properties Manager (in a wheelchair) meets with the group on property issues.	11:30 – 14:28
NOTES:	

Questions for Discussion

1. Although not required by their job description why do Pam and Ryan both refuse to pick up Michael? Why is this so? Should they have picked him up? What would be the benefits? What would be the negative outcomes of doing so?

   Common courtesy might suggest that Pam and/or Ryan go pick up Michael at home; however, it is important that they somehow not set up the expectation that they will complete such tasks that are so far outside of their job descriptions. This is especially important for Ryan who as a "temp" has few defined duties. But this is a double-edged sword of sorts as he may want to manage his impression with Michael to leverage against getting a full-time position.

2. Michael continually makes outrageous requests of his employees, especially Ryan "The Temp". Why does Michael treat Ryan this way? Is it ok to treat him this way since he is not a permanent employee? What sort of norm would this create the office? This sends a specific message to the other employees about the treatment of different "levels" of employees?

   Michael continues to marginalize the contribution of Ryan. As a non-permanent employee with few specific job duties Ryan has little recourse for Michael's requests. By treating him this way Michael has set the expectation that it is "ok" to treat temporary workers such as Ryan poorly. This is a dangerous precedent to set and could impact the office negatively.

3. Michael brings in the property manager to talk about "disability issues" without his knowledge. Even if we assume that he was informed of Michael's intent, is this an appropriate way to

demonstrate issues with individuals with disabilities? What might be a better way?

The tactic of bringing in someone with a disability in order to show that they are capable of performing different tasks might be an effective way to demonstrate these concepts to some employees. To determine if this is the proper way to send his intended message, managers such as Michael should have intricate knowledge of what their employees respond well to and match their programming to these styles.

ROBERT G. DELCAMPO, PH.D., KRISTIE M. BOUDWIN and SHERRI L. HINES

THE OFFICE
SEASON TWO

Episode 2–13 The Secret

Summary: Jim is concerned that Michael will share Jim's secret feelings for Pam with the rest of the office. He is so desperate to keep Michael quiet that he agrees to go to lunch with him. They have lunch at Hooters, and Michael has a great time. He reveals the secret sparking office gossip. Jim tells Pam about the crush but makes it seem that it was a long time ago. Dwight was given the responsibility to investigate Oscar to find out if he was truly sick.

Topics: Trust, Workplace Deviance, Appropriate Workplace Behavior

Clip Description	Start/Stop
Today is spring cleaning day, and Oscar is out sick. Michael called him at home and asks for his symptoms. He assigns Dwight to investigate.	2:41 – 4:02
Michael makes an inappropriate comment to Pam regarding her hair and a comment to Jim. Jim asked Michael to keep the information regarding his feelings toward Pam a secret.	4:03 – 5:40
Michael invites Jim to lunch who reluctantly accepts. He takes Jim to Hooters. Michael explains that he likes Hooters for the "boobs and the hotwings."	8:30 – 10:09
At lunch, Michael tries to get Jim to open up about Pam. Michael makes inappropriate comments.	10:38 – 11:26
The secret is out, and the entire office is talking. When Jim discovers that everyone knows, he decides to tell Pam about the conversation with Michael. He confesses his feelings and tries to make it look like it was in the past.	14:14 – 16:29
Dwight has been waiting for Oscar to get him and discovers Oscar's secret. Dwight does not realize that Oscar is gay.	16:30 - 17:51

NOTES:

Questions for Discussion

1. Jim has shared his personal feelings for Pam with Michael. While Michael is obviously not the best person to exchange this information with, what are the inherent problems with disclosing personal information to one's boss? Are there any positive ramifications to self-disclosure of this nature? How would this impact the relationship?

    Once again, self-disclosure is a double-edged sword. While it builds a strong bond between co-workers and promotes trust, it can create a certain level of discomfort and in-turn reduced productivity in the workplace.

2. Is it appropriate for Michael to take Jim to lunch at Hooters? Is there any situation in which this would be appropriate? How does the power differential between Michael and Jim impact Jim's ability to decline the invitation?

    Opinions will vary greatly on this topic. Gender issues are important to discuss in relation to this topic. Be sure that comments are non-judgmental, developmental and constructive.

3. Michael does not believe that Oscar is truly sick. Why might Oscar be faking his sickness? Why do employees engage in counterproductive work behaviors such as this? What are some others?

    From time to time, employees will do things like "act sick", steal office supplies, make personal phone calls or even commit fraud or steal from work. They normally engage in these activities to "even the pot" or create equity in their work arrangement. These employees normally view themselves as under-

> rewarded and take additional time off or resources from the office and rationalize their actions by using the concept of inequity to morally disengage from this type of behavior that they would normally view as inappropriate.

4. The faking of sickness is a common employee "ailment", how might a benefit program be constructed that keeps sick employees home but does not encourage misuse of paid sick leave?

   > Responses to this question might include on-site health care, paying out a percentage of unused sick leave a prescribed time, etc.

5. Suppose Oscar is truly sick. If he were to come into work, how would that impact the rest of the office? Would productivity be hindered? What are the other ramifications of presenteeism?

   > Presenteeism is as serious of an issue as absenteeism. Sick employees coming to work can very seriously impact the productivity of the workplace by getting others sick, creating anxiety that others will get sick or even as simply as creating a reduced level of work output by the sick employee. Sick employees sometimes view themselves as committed if they show up to work, but in reality they can do more harm than good.

6. Michael sends Dwight to "investigate" if Oscar is truly sick. Is this an acceptable task to request? What are the problems with requesting such a task? How would this impact the relationship between Michael and Oscar if he were to find out?

   > Michael and Oscar could have a severe trust crisis if Oscar was truly sick. An interesting line of inquiry might be the value of Michael doubting Oscar's

sickness. If Oscar is an employee who has earned this sick time why should he judge how or when it is used? What rights does he have to do so? It seems that some managers would view this leave time as something earned and not question its use.

THE OFFICE
SEASON TWO

Episode 2–14 The Carpet

Summary: Michael arrives at the office to discover that a very foul smelling item has been left on the carpet in his office. He is desperate to find out who would ruin a perfectly fine carpet and thinks it could be a hate crime or an act of terrorism. While the carpet is being replaced, he takes over Jim's desk forcing Jim to find temporary space in the back of the office with Kelly. Michael and Dwight replay office pranks pulled by Michael and Packer years before.

Topics: Extra-Role Behavior, Trust, Psychological Contracts, Employee Discipline

Clip Description	Start/Stop
Pam is on vacation and Ryan is sitting at her desk. Jim misses Pam and stares at Ryan. Ryan states that Jim has been staring at him all week, but at least he doesn't look at him the way Michael does.	0:00 – 0:53
Michael questions Pam about her vacation and asks if she got lucky. He discovers a foul smelling item in his office and sends Kevin in to identify the object and will not let him out.	1:26 – 3:12
Michael reminisces about office pranks with Todd Packer. Michael roams the office harassing the employees.	6:34 – 7:30
Michael and Dwight raid Accounting and trash the area. The clip includes Michael's belief that the foul smelling object was an act of terrorism against the office.	8:12 – 9:53
Michael believes he is the victim of a hate crime, and the crime was committed by someone in the office. He claims that Stanley knows what it is like to be a victim of a hate crime. Everyone is put on "time out."	13:17 – 14:39
NOTES:	

Questions for Discussion

1. Michael is upset with the "prank" that has been pulled on him. How does this influence his interaction with the people in the office throughout the day? Does this underlying resentment impact productivity? How else might he approach being upset but still allowing the office to function properly?

    Michael has created a climate of distrust by his questioning of employees about the prank. Obviously, most employees would be uncomfortable in this situation of being questioned and second-guessed and either consciously or sub-consciously would have their productivity impacted.

2. Michael believes he is the victim of a hate crime. He then puts the entire office in a "time out". What might be a better way to approach the situation with his workers? Has this crisis damaged the trust that exists between Michael and his workers and vice versa? How would this crisis of trust impact the way the employees interact with Michael knowing now that he does not trust their words (that they didn't commit the prank)?

    Michael's choice of "time out" is obviously demeaning to his employees. The concept of punishing everyone if no one will confess is a bit juvenile and obviously not the best way to approach the situation. If surveillance is available, Michael might investigate video tape to determine the culprit or simply not acknowledge the behavior at all. As a manager it is his prerogative to decide how to reinforce or punish this behavior, but his action should be congruent with the values, wants and needs of his employees. The understanding of employee values, wants and needs is not only necessary for rewarding, but also for punishing employees.

3. Michael has a history of pranking people at work. Although he hasn't changed his ways since becoming Regional Manager, should he? What would be both the positive and negative ramifications of changing his behavior at work? What liability does this present for Dunder Mifflin?

   With his history of pranking people at Dunder Mifflin, Michael's credibility in getting angry with his "pranker" is severely limited. He should understand that his past behavior will influence his future treatment and realize that he has set a precedent for what is/is not acceptable. In terms of liability, management is responsible for implementing policy, and Dunder Mifflin should take steps to insure that Michael is aware of their policies.

THE OFFICE
SEASON TWO

Episode 2–15 Boys and Girls

Summary: Jan is in Scranton to conduct a "Women in the Workplace" seminar. Michael hates not being included and decides to conduct his own seminar for the "boys." His session is held in the warehouse. It turns into a gripe session and talk of unionizing. Michael unsuccessfully attempts to diffuse the situation. Jan encourages Pam to attend the company's Design Training Program to develop her drawing skills.

Topics: Training and Development, Cross-Gender Relations, Stereotypes, Employee Reward Systems, Organized Labor/Unions

Clip Description	Start/Stop
Michael is unhappy about Jan talking in secret with all the women. He addresses the women and shares his idea of the Ally McBeal woman.	0:00 – 1:37
Dwight thinks it's a terrible idea to have all the women in the same room together because they will get on the same cycle.	2:12 – 2:36
The clip includes introductions of the warehouse staff. He makes several inappropriate comments regarding stereotypes. Michael shares that he does not see blue collar and white collar employees because he is collar blind.	4:44 – 6:05
Michael discovers a blowup sex doll in the warehouse with a copy of Michael's face taped over the doll face.	7:29 – 8:00
Guys gripe session. The talk turns to unionization, and Michael inadvertently shows support. When Ryan suggests an assembly line for more efficiency, Stanley tells him the work is on the "run out the clock".	11:49 – 14:40
Michael trashes the warehouse. He orders pizza because pizza is the great equalizer, rich or poor, white or black. He wonders aloud if black people like pizza. He also shares his philosophy as to why an office needs men and women – the crazy sexual tension.	18:55 – 20:18
NOTES:	

"THAT'S WHAT SHE SAID!"

Questions for Discussion

1. Why is it "ok" for Jan to run a "women in the workplace" seminar but not "ok" for Michael to have a "men in the workplace" seminar? How is this indicative of the underlying gender bias in today's workplace? Do seminars like this help or hurt the plight of women at work?

    a. *Once again, it will be interesting to hear the differing viewpoints of students on these issues. Gender bias is a difficult issue to navigate sometimes and creates strong feelings on both sides. It is especially interesting to highlight the idea that seminars like this may actually do more harm than good as they create even deeper divisions between male and female employees.*

2. During the "gripe session" Michael is present for some talk of unionization of the office workers. How do you think he handled this situation? What are the benefits of working with organized labor? The costs?

    a. *Dealing with organized labor is a slippery issue at best. From the standpoint of the employees it appears to be an ideal solution; however management sees this as an opportunity for increased labor costs and difficulty for the future. Michael should more than likely remove himself from this conversation and allow the employees to discuss such issues without him present. While there are strict legal (which in some cases vary on a state-to-state basis) constraints and who, when and where organizing issues can be discussed, in order to keep himself in the good graces of upper management and the employees it might be best for Michael to step out of this conversation.*

3. Michael says that pizza is "the great equalizer". Does a simple reward such as pizza really diffuse the situation? What other types of "minor" rewards could help to improve employee morale and job satisfaction?

   a. *Student responses will vary. It is important to note the sometimes wide sweeping impact of the "little things" at work. Sometimes unexpected rewards or opportunities to relax are the more effective tools to improve the work environment. Note that some student responses will be more realistic than others (in regard to cost, feasibility, etc.)*

THE OFFICE
SEASON TWO

Episode 2–16 Valentine's Day

Summary: It's Valentine's Day, and the majority of the staff is happily participating in the festivities. Michael is in New York City to make a presentation to the new CFO of Dunder Mifflin. He tells the other participants about his relationship with Jan which leads to a major problem when the CFO is made aware of the same. Back at the office, the issue of holiday gifts poses problems for almost everyone.

Topics: Workplace Romance, Performance Appraisal, Impression Management

Clip Description	Start/Stop
Michael and the other managers talk about Jan, and he slips and tells them about hooking up with her.	9:35 – 10:20
Jan is nervous about the meeting with the new CFO. Michael's presentation is a short film about the employees of the Scranton branch. He introduces Stanley, an African-American father of two, and also points out that Pam is very cute—not bad at all.	11:23 – 14:45
The meeting continues. Craig did not bring any numbers to the meeting and makes the comment that he should have slept with Jan to avoid trouble. Jan could possibly lose her job because of it, and they did not even sleep together.	15:45 – 17:31
Dwight shares his very interesting ideas about women—that women are like wolves and need to be treated as such.	17:32 – 18:00
NOTES:	

Questions for Discussion:

1. Michael prepares a lengthy presentation for the new CFO. It appears that this presentation does not have the type of information that was expected; however, why would Michael want to present this "side" of his employees? Should this sort of introduction be welcomed? Why would it be important for the CFO to know about the "people in Scranton"?

    a. *While Michael's presentation wasn't exactly what the CFO was looking for, he is attempting to somehow "humanize" the people in his office. This way he can get the corporate office to understand that the employees in his office are more than just "numbers" by attaching a face and a name to a position. Perhaps Michael should have presented this information in a more succinct manner and ALSO include the necessary financial information in order to balance the needs of corporate and his desire to present his employees.*

2. Michael discloses to his colleagues that he "hooked up" with Jan. What might have been a more appropriate (or HR-compliant) way of disclosing this information?

    a. *Most companies have policies in place for disclosing office relationships. While this relationship has not progressed to a state where it is long-term it may be in Michael's best interest to discreetly disclose this information to an HR representative so that it may be noted and help him avoid any negative outcomes that could be associated with such a situation.*

3. At the end of the episode, Dwight shares his misogynistic view of women. How prevalent do you think this view really is? Can

someone with these types of views really be "changed"? How would you manage someone working with a woman that holds similar views?

   a. *Student responses will vary. It is interesting to note the differing opinions about whether or not strongly held (yet somewhat socially unacceptable) views such as this can be changed. It is important to bring up the concept that diversity training/awareness programs are implement to attempt to do just this—change views, or are they? Bring up the issue that sometimes awareness is the best we can accomplish. Even if we cannot change views, we can at least make individuals aware of the fact that such controversial viewpoints should not be shared in the workplace.*

THE OFFICE
SEASON TWO

Episode 2–17 Dwight's Speech

Summary: Dwight has been named the Dunder Mifflin Salesman of the Year and must give an acceptance speech at the company convention. He is terrified of public speaking and enlists the help of Michael and Jim. Jim is busy making plans to be out of town for Pam's wedding and enlists the help of the entire office to figure out where to vacation. The accounting staff is in the middle of a thermostat control battle.

Topics: Power and Political Behavior, Impression Management, Motivation

Clip Description	Start/Stop
Throwing a football helps Michael think, and the game gets out of hand. Dwight tackles Ryan and pushes him to the ground.	0:00 - 1:16
Funny example of an attempt at an inappropriate comment. Dwight goes to Michael for assistance with his convention speech. Michael's help includes horrible comments about Dwight's lack of skill and ability.	3:16 - 5:13
The public speaking lesson continues with an inappropriate joke. He makes a false announcement that everyone is getting a bonus and assigns Dwight the task of cleaning up the mess.	5:59 - 8:25
Michael is filling in for Dwight at the convention until Dwight is able to address the crowd. Thankfully, Dwight finds his courage and makes his speech (Mussolini's War Statement). The clip ends with Dwight laughing like a crazy man.	15:17 - 17:21

NOTES:

Questions for Discussion:

1. Dwight has been awarded "Salesman of the Year," however he is still not taken seriously in the Dunder Mifflin-Scranton office. Why is this so? How could he better represent himself to gain respect?

    a. *While Dwight is a high-performing employee he still lacks credibility in the office. This could perhaps be due to the fact that his sales acumen has led to him taking on more administrative tasks for which he has no specific expertise (i.e., his role as "Assistant to the Regional Manager). It should be noted that many times people are promoted (see information on "The Peter Principle") to a different area based on their expertise in a different, unrelated area. To improve his level of esteem in the office it might be best for Dwight to stick to the sales tasks that he performs well.*

2. Michael delegates the task of telling the office that they will not be getting a bonus to Dwight. What sorts of problems will this cause? How will it impact productivity? Do the employees have any legal recourse?

    a. *In terms of legal recourse it is difficult to say what the employees might be able to do, however ethically this is definitely a poor decision. Michael basically makes Dwight the "bad guy" in this (as he does many times) case. While no one likes to deliver bad news, the ability and responsibility to do so lies with the manager (in this case) and can actually build credibility among employees even though the news may not be what they want to hear.*

3. Public speaking is an important skill in many different occupations. Michael attempts to "teach" people about how to overcome their fear of speaking in public, however unsuccessfully. Do you believe that public speaking is a useful skill in all professions? Why/why not? How can one improve their ability to speak in public?

   a. *Human relations expertise in general is a great skill in any profession. Included in this expertise is the ability to speak in public. While some professions do not lend themselves directly to the need for public speaking/human relations expertise it can only enhance their ability to be productive and upwardly mobile. For example, the accountant who can also talk to the client comfortably will be able to recruit new clients and grow the business, thus making them more likely to move into management. In terms of improving public speaking/human relations skills many training/coaching programs exist and should be investigated to improve these skills for those interested.*

THE OFFICE
SEASON TWO

Episode 2–18 Take Your Daughter To Work Day

Summary: Today is "Take Your Daughter To Work Day" and several of the staff have brought in their children. Michael acknowledges and demonstrates that he is not very good around children. Pam is also inexperienced and has a goal of making one child like her. Michael bonds with Toby's daughter and finds himself interested in entertaining the children.

Topics: Work-Life Balance, Appropriate Workplace Behavior, Employee Morale and Motivation

Clip Description	Start/Stop
Pam reminds Michael that he cannot be nasty today because it is Take Your Daughter To Work Day. Michael explains that the office is more like HBO, R rated rather than G.	0:00 – 1:28
Michael meets Stanley's daughter and refers to her as a "stone cold fox," and Stanley lets him know that she is in the 8th grade.	2:48 – 3:20
Stanley's daughter Melissa takes a liking to Ryan making Kelly very jealous. Kelly tells Stanley that something fishy is going on causing Stanley to yell at Ryan.	7:44 – 8:39
Michael signs up with an on-line dating service. He chooses a user name of "little kid lover" so that way people will know exactly where his priorities lie.	18:02 – 18:26

NOTES:

"THAT'S WHAT SHE SAID!"

Questions for Discussion:

1. "Take Your Daughter To Work Day" has become more and more popular over the past few years. What is the reasoning behind such an event? Does it work?

    a. *Student responses will vary. It is interesting to hear their views on this issue. It should be noted that they idea behind "Take Your Daughter to Work Day" is to provide positive role modeling for young women as well as create dialogue between daughters and parents.*

2. Is it appropriate to bring one's children to work? What are the potential problems? What about liability for the company?

    a. *Many companies have policies surrounding children entering the workplace, and for good reason. Again, responses will vary but it is important to note what an organization might "like to allow" and what they "can/should allow".*

3. Programs such as taking one's daughter to work certainly have some benefit, but also cost the company a great deal in lost productivity and efficiency. What would be the ramifications of not allowing employees to participate in a program like this? Would it be "worth it"? Why/why not? What are some other public relations oriented decisions that are made that can have similar results?

    a. *Once again, responses will vary however the negative public relations slant on outwardly disallowing employees to participate in such a program should be noted. It is blanker statements like this that become flash point issues for the media and could possibly end up being more "expensive" (from a PR standpoint) in the future. It is important to weigh all ramifications of such a program before making any judgments about the viability of implementing them.*

THE OFFICE
SEASON TWO

Episode 2–19 Michael's Birthday

Summary: Today is Michael's birthday, and he has several things planned to celebrate the day. Unfortunately, the entire staff is more interested in comforting Kevin who is waiting for results from a medical test to determine if he has skin cancer. Michael becomes angry at the lack of attention. Once he is made aware of the situation, he becomes more sympathetic yet remains determined to make the most of his birthday by taking everyone to a skating rink.

Topics: Employee Health and Welfare, Employee Morale, Employee Reward Systems, Appropriate Workplace Behavior

Clip Description	**Start/Stop**
The party planning committee is informed that Michael wants a stripper-gram for his birthday.	3:52 – 4:30
Michael mistakes a delivery person for a stripper. He slips money into her front pocket and then takes Dwight's chair and drags it into the center of the room. The chair has armrests, and Michael asks if that will be a problem.	6:41 – 7:20
The romantic interaction between Angela and Dwight makes Ryan very uncomfortable, and he is rendered speechless.	11:53 – 12:44
Michael tries to cheer Kevin up, and when that doesn't work, tells him to go home. Michael is trying to salvage his birthday and takes the staff to a staking rink. The clip includes Michael crashing into people and cutting in front of others. Finally, Michael advises Pam to give herself an exam next time she is in the shower because "those things are like ticking time bags."	15:09 – 18:03

NOTES:

"THAT'S WHAT SHE SAID!"

Questions for Discussion:

1. Michael mentions to Pam that she needs to "give herself an exam". This is obviously inappropriate, however the sentiment may be genuine. What might be a better way of communicating this sort of message to his employees?

    a. *If Michael's true objective is employee health and welfare, rather than give crude and inappropriate directives he might investigate and start a comprehensive wellness program in the office. It has been noted that the existence and use of employee wellness programs not only improves job satisfaction but also productivity and can curb turnover and absenteeism.*

2. Kevin has a cancer scare during this episode, what sort of opportunity does this provide the office in terms of awareness? How does one deal with an employee going through a similar or even more serious situation? Is Michael's remedy of just sending him home effective? What might be better?

    a. *See above. Michael's idea to "send him home" is not the most effective form of dealing with the situation. While in the short term it removes the immediate concern for Kevin from the office (and potentially creates a return to productivity) it send the message of "out of sight, out of mind" therein creating a culture of disinterest in employee wellness.*

3. Kevin shares his concern about a soon-to-be-revealed medical test to his co-workers. Is this something you would do? Why/why not? How do you balance having friends as co-workers? Is there certain information that is necessary to withhold? Where is that line drawn?

a. *Student responses will vary. This affords the opportunity for an in-depth discussion about boundaries. It is interesting to note that different students will have different ideas about the information they are comfortable sharing and that information that they are not comfortable sharing. Note these differences in class as well as the fact that these varied opinions more than likely exist in the workplace.*

THE OFFICE
SEASON TWO

Episode 2–20 Drug Testing

Summary: Dwight has found half of a joint in the company parking lot and, because he is a Lackawanna County Volunteer Sheriff's Deputy, feels he is duty bound to solve the crime and identify the criminal. He interrogates employees and makes arrangements to have everyone tested for drugs (per company policy.) Michael convinces Dwight to give him "clean urine" for his test because Michael may have accidentally gotten high at an Alicia Keys concert.

Topics: Employee Rights and Discipline, Leadership, Workplace Drug Testing

Clip Description	Start/Stop
Dwight finds half a joint and is determined to find the guilty party. This clip shows Kevin's interrogation—he seems to meet the profile of someone who smokes marijuana.	0:00 – 1:06
Dwight continues his harassment of employees. Michael wants him to "chill out" but Dwight believes the investigation is his job. Michael begins calling him names and generally making fun.	2:33 – 4:13
The interrogation continues with interviews and Jim turning the tables and conducting an interview with Dwight.	5:11 – 5:54
Dwight made arrangements for drug testing per company policy. Michael is very concerned because he was exposed to drugs at a concert. Dwight continues asking illegal questions about employee prescription drug use.	7:16 – 9:10
An office meeting is held to discuss the evils of drugs. The clip includes an interesting list of "drugs," and Michael threatening to test hair and blood. Michael does not want to be tested.	9:45 – 13:55
Michael requests Dwight's urine for the test. Dwight is conflicted because it is illegal.	14:15 – 16:59

NOTES:

"THAT'S WHAT SHE SAID!"

Questions for Discussion:

1. Dwight and Michael decide to test everyone in the office for drugs stating that it conforms to company policy. While conventional wisdom would dictate that drug testing is a "good" idea, are their any instances (different job types, different industries) in which drug testing might be counterproductive? Why?

    a. *While using illegal drugs is in no way excusable, the cost for testing all employees can be quite costly. Additionally, students might note that some (albeit irresponsible) employers might not want to know or even care if their employees are drug users (for example, it is well noted that truck drivers have a culture of stimulant use that is regulated but is 'overlooked' by many). Again, this is not an excuse for drug use but merely an attempt to examine the realistic side of drug testing.*

2. In one of these instances where drug testing might be counterproductive, is there any added corporate liability by not testing the employees?

    a. *See above. It should also be noted that liability does absolutely fall upon the company in many cases where employees use drugs on the job.*

3. Dwight interrogates each employee in the office about the marijuana found in the parking lot. Is this an effective strategy to determine who the culprit might be? What might be a better strategy for determining who is guilty?

    a. *Students may note that the concept of trust is of key importance here. As in many instances in "The Office", 'dis-trust' seems to be the default assumption. Rather than spend a large amount of*

> *time interrogating employees it may be more productive to allow a guilty employee to come forward under the directive that there will be no punishment. Additionally, trusting the word of each employee should be accepted at some point.*

4. Michael refuses to take the drug test citing his fear that he may test positive. If this was a new policy, (be it drug testing, a new voluntary procedure, etc.), why/why shouldn't Michael be the first to submit? What sort of message does this send to the other employees? Is this an effective leadership strategy?

   a. *In this case (and in others too) setting an example is key to gaining employee buy in. While Michael is somewhat reviled and at best tolerated by his employees by being the first to volunteer or submit to a policy or procedure he sends a message to the employees that this is not only "ok" but "a good thing". Key to adoption or acceptance of any change in an organization is the buy in of management, if their support is not gained the objective is sure to fail.*

THE OFFICE
SEASON TWO

Episode 2–21 Conflict Resolution

Summary: Staff is now required to wear photo badges and a photographer is in the office taking pictures. Michael overhears Toby counseling Oscar regarding a dispute with Angela. Michael is not pleased with Toby's conflict resolution style and takes over the task. His rather unorthodox style creates numerous problems and ill-will with the entire staff. Meanwhile, Pam is carrying out her wedding planning on office time causing additional problems with a certain co-worker.

Topics: Conflict, Power and Politics, Employee Privacy, Employee Rights and Discipline, Leadership

Clip Description	Start/Stop
Today is photo day. The clip includes Dwight upsetting Phyllis, Michael invading Ryan's space and touching his clothes making Ryan very uncomfortable. Michael takes over conflict resolution from Toby and mediates the conflict between Angela and Oscar.	1:21 – 6:05
Michael forces Toby to hand over the conflict files to review and get everything out into the open for resolution. It is revealed that Dwight has a standing meeting with Toby every Friday to file a grievance against Jim with the grievance going to a special box in New York.	6:30 – 11:38
Michael continues to mediate disputes between Angela and Phyllis; Creed and Ryan; and Angela and Kevin. Angela complained that Kevin made sexual remarks to her. Michael suggests that Angela make sexual remarks to Kevin. Dwight discovers that his complaints against Jim have not been handled.	12:10 – 14:42
Michael mediates between Dwight and Jim, and they go over the list of complaints. Michael's approach is that of a "cage match," and he explains his philosophy. Jim notes that the pranks do not sound as funny when they are revealed one after another.	15:58 – 16:37
NOTES:	

"THAT'S WHAT SHE SAID!"

Questions for Discussion:

1. Michael takes over conflict resolution responsibilities in the office. Is this a "good idea"? Why/why not? Why is conflict resolution generally the responsibility of a Human Resources representative? How does this alienate this individual (as many tasks do for Toby)?

    a. *By "taking over" the conflict resolution responsibilities in the office Michael has put himself in a very difficult position. It is to avoid situations such as this that HR representatives are placed in branch offices such as Dunder Mifflin-Scranton. By taking over this task Michael sends the message that Toby is not only incompetent (in his view) but unimportant. Addtionally, Michael is placed in a no-win situation where he will almost certainly alienate certain employees (not to mention that he most likely has no specific training in conflict resolution).*

2. Toby places Dwight's complains about Jim in a "special file in New York" which is actually a box that he never addresses. What are the potential ramifications of doing this? Even if the complaints are unfounded what is Toby's responsibility to investigate them? Should he dismiss complaints that seem groundless?

    a. *While humorous, it is a grave error to not properly address employee complaints no matter how frivolous. If any legal action were to come about as a result of these complains Dunder Mifflin and Toby himself would be placed in a very difficult situation. By ignoring all complaints by Dwight, Toby may inadvertently dismiss a valid complaint at some point in the future.*

3. Michael mediates multiple disputes in this episode with varying degrees of success. While his methods are somewhat questionable he does do some things correctly. What does he do correctly? What could he do differently?

   a. *Michael does many things correctly such as attempting to find "new" or novel ways to resolve disputes, getting both parties together to discuss the issues, allowing both parties to talk, etc. However, there are many things that Michael could do differently (i.e., not interrupting, etc.). Student responses will vary.*

"THAT'S WHAT SHE SAID!"

THE OFFICE
SEASON TWO

Episode 2–22 Casino Night

Summary: Tonight is Dunder Mifflin's charity casino night being held in the warehouse now transformed to a Monte Carlo nightclub. Whoever has the most chips at the end of the night will receive $500 to donate to a charity of their choosing. Michael ends up with two dates for the event, and Dwight assists by keeping the women apart. Pam is trying to choose a band to play at the wedding reception, and Jim is considering a transfer to the Stanford branch.

Topics: Appropriate Workplace Behavior, Diversity, Employee Rights and Discipline

Clip Description	Start/Stop
Michael announces that the charity check will be given to an actual Boy Scout at Casino Night. Toby explains why it is not appropriate—in a dangerous warehouse, alcohol on the premises, and catering courtesy of Hooters. Michael gets assistance from the office in choosing a charity.	5:30 – 7:15
Michael wants fire eaters in the warehouse. Dwight came to the office to protect him from Daryl. Daryl explains how he has helped Michael out with "things that Negroes say" to improve his race conversations.	8:10 – 9:17
This clip highlights Creed and his love of stealing things. Michael tells Billy that his nurse is hot—she is his girlfriend. He then proceeds to welcome "old friends, new lovers, and the disabled."	14:11 – 16:52

NOTES:

Questions for Discussion:

1. Toby acts as the "voice of reason" many times. As the HR representative at the Scranton branch, he is reviled by Michael and some of the other employees. Is this common for HR officers? How does/can he better balance the varied goals of corporate and the branch? Is he in a no-win situation?

    a. *Students will note that there are many conflicting demands for HR representatives. They are somewhat marginalized by corporate headquarters and by their office location (in situations similar to Toby's). While difficult, it is important for HR to maintain a neutral stance in inter- and intra-office matters. While it may not be "fun" they are meant to maintain a somewhat neutral position in corporate politics.*

2. Daryl "helps" Michael to relate to some of his employees. Had Michael truly felt that he was having difficulty relating to his employees what might be a better strategy to do this? Can these sorts of behaviors truly be learned?

    a. *Michael is quite obviously not particularly skilled in relating to his employees. While his attempts to "get to their level" are admirable there are other tactics that might be more effective. Students will note that it is also necessary sometimes for the "boss" to maintain different types of relationships with their employees than those shared among the bulk of the office workers. Of key importance is to note the importance of effectively and actively listening to employee needs, wants and interests.*

3. Dunder Mifflin chooses to have a charity fundraiser to help a deserving charity. What are the potential benefits/detriments in

choosing particular charities to benefit from the work of one's company? Make a list of non-profit organizations and the pros/cons of each. Do you think companies do this in deciding "who" should benefit from their efforts? Should they? Does this defeat the purpose of raising charity funds?

    a. *The concept of raising funds or interest in a particular cause is difficult to manage, while raising funds for charity is admirable and many times a large component in corporate social responsibility, it is important to note that there are sometimes larger political implications when donating money to particular institutions. Organizations should examine what sort of "message" donating to certain non-profit organizations might send. This applies especially when considering socially stratified issues or politically charged issues and the charities associated with them.*

Bibliography

BBC. Retrieved August 23, 2007, from http://www.bbc.co.uk

Champoux, J. (2001). Animated films as a teaching resource. Journal of Management Education, 25: 79-100.

Christensen, C., Garvin, D. & Sweet, A. (1991). Education for judgment. Boston, MA: Harvard Business School.

Corner, D. (2001). Not just a Mickey Mouse exercise: Using Disney's The Lion King to teach leadership. Journal of Management Education, 25: 430-436.

Huczynski, A. (1994). Teaching motivation and influencing strategies using The Magnificent Seven. Journal of Management Education, 18: 273-278.

Hunt, C. (2001). Must see TV: The timelessness of television as a teaching tool. Journal of Management Education, 25: 631-647.

Merchant, S. & Gervais, R. (Executive Producers). (2005). The Office [Television series]. New York: National Broadcasting Company.

Index

ADA 84
Appropriate Workplace Behavior
    28, 40, 52, 60, 68, 76, 88, 109, 113, 125
Communication 44, 52, 64, 68, 72, 80, 84
Conflict, Power and Politics ... 121
Co-worker harassment 16
Cross-Gender Relations 97
Cultural Sensitivity 20
Development 97
Diversity 20, 22, 23, 31, 40, 84, 125
Downsizing... 7, 16, 17, 28, 56, 58
Electronic Monitoring 44, 72
E-Mail Surveillance 72
Employee Benefits 24
Employee Discipline 93
Employee Feedback 68
Employee Health and Welfare 113
Employee Privacy 72, 121
Employee Recognition 40
Employee Reward Systems 34, 97, 113
Employee Rights and Discipline
    .... 117, 121, 125
Employee Termination 56
Equal Opportunity 52
Equity Theory 76
Extra-Role Behavior.... 24, 31, 34, 48, 84, 93
Fairness 68
Gender Issues 28, 52
Impression Management 101, 105
Incentives 34

Job Descriptions 48, 68
Job Satisfaction 24, 40, 48, 56
Job Security 16, 56
Leadership 80, 117, 121
Managerial Decision Making 56
Managing Work Flows 60
Mentoring 52
Morale 24, 28, 40, 48, 56, 109, 113
Motivation.. 24, 34, 40, 48, 76, 80, 105, 109
OCB 24, 48, 84
Office Romance 34, 60, 64, 68, 72
Organizational culture 16
Organized Labor/Unions 97
Outside of work relationships ... 72
Performance Appraisal 68, 101
Peter Principle 64, 67
Power and Political Behavior .. 105
Psychological Contracts 24, 48, 76, 93
Recognition and Rewards ... 76, 80
Sexual Harassment. 16, 44, 46, 47, 62
Stereotypes 20, 31, 97
Team Building .. 31, 40, 48, 56, 80
Teams 80
Training 44, 97
Trust 88, 93
Work Environment 20
Work-Life Balance 24, 48, 109
Workplace Deviance 88
Workplace Privacy 64
Workplace Romance 101
Workplace Safety and Health ... 52

Printed in the United States
144179LV00001B/6/A